Reading Aboriginal Women's Life Stories

Anne Brewster

SYDNEY UNIVERSITY PRESS

Published by Sydney University Press
© Anne Brewster 2015
© Sydney University Press 2015

First published as *Reading Aboriginal Women's Autobiography* in Melbourne in 1996 by Oxford University Press, in association with Sydney University Press.

This book was written on land traditionally owned by the Nyoongah people and produced on land traditionally owned by the Gadigal people of the Eora nation.

Reproduction and Communication for other purposes
Except as permitted under the Act, no part of this edition may be reproduced, stored in a retrieval system, or communicated in any form or by any means without prior written permission. All requests for reproduction or communication should be made to Sydney University Press at the address below:

Sydney University Press
Fisher Library F03
University of Sydney NSW 2006
AUSTRALIA
sup.info@sydney.edu.au
sydney.edu.au/sup

National Library of Australia Cataloguing-in-Publication Data

Author:	Anne Brewster
Title:	Reading Aboriginal Women's Life Stories
ISBN:	9781743324189 (paperback)
	9781743324196 (ebook: epub)
	9781743324202 (ebook: mobipocket)
Notes:	Includes bibliographical references
Subjects:	Autobiography--Women authors.
	Women, Aboriginal Australian--Biography--History and criticism.
	Aboriginal Australians--Social conditions.
	Australian literature--20th century--History and criticism.
	Australian literature--Aboriginal authors--History and criticism.
Dewey Number:	A820.9492072

Cover image: an illustration based on Aboriginal style of dot painting depicting snake skin, image 172953698 by dedoma, used under license from Shutterstock.com

Cover design by Miguel Yamin

Contents

Foreword   v

Acknowledgements   vii

Note on Authors' Names   ix

Introduction   xi

1. Aboriginality and Sally Morgan's *My Place*   1
2. Issues of Race and Gender in Ruby Langford's *Don't Take Your Love To Town*   19
3. Family and Storytelling in Alice Nannup's *When The Pelican Laughed*   35

Works Cited   47

Foreword

My copy of *Reading Aboriginal Women's Autobiography* is deeply familiar: its scuffed cover records the many times I have pulled this book off the shelf, carried it to tutorials and lectures, and marked up passages and quotations in pencil, pen, and fluoro markers. This book opens up ways of reading Indigenous women's life writing with care and respect. Looking back, we can recognise now what an extraordinary phenomenon these life stories are, and how they have changed understandings of Aboriginality and writing. This book reminds me that I needed to learn to read this writing, to understand and respect its difference, and lived experiences of Aboriginality. The return of this classic book in a new edition is a welcome reminder that Anne Brewster's careful, deeply respectful and informed approach to these writings is as necessary now as it ever was. This new revised edition, *Reading Aboriginal Women's Life Stories*, is a guide to what we now recognise as a new country in Australian literature, in women's writing, and in world literature.

Professor Gillian Whitlock FAHA

Acknowledgements

I would like to thank Rosemary van den Berg, Doris Pilkington, Sally Morgan and Darlene Oxenham for reading sections of this book in the 1992 manuscript form and for their advice and comments.

Note on Authors' Names

Several of the writers discussed in this book have written under different names: *Ruby Langford* has appeared in recent publications as Ruby Langford Ginibi; *Roberta Sykes* published her earlier work under the name Bobbi Sykes; and *Mudrooroo* has published variously under the names Colin Johnson, Mudrooroo Narogin, Mudrooroo Nyoongah and Mudrooroo. In the text they are referred to by the names italicised in this note; in the Bibliography their works are listed under these names.

Introduction

> we're talkin' history
> Arthur Corunna (Morgan, 1987: 163)

Aboriginal people have often been called the most socially and economically disadvantaged group in Australia. As Ruby Langford says:

> We Kooris are fifteen to twenty years behind everyone else in all the basic human rights such as health, housing, employment and education; even the people who migrate here are on a higher social level than we are, and we're the first people of this land! My people were forced to give away using our language and culture, and adopt the ways of the white man. (Langford, 1994d: 52)

Sometimes Australian culture is described as 'postcolonial', in the sense that Australia is a Commonwealth and no longer made up of British colonies. This term also implies that, having become independent, Australia has largely left its 'colonial' history behind. But Australia's role as a coloniser/invader continues, as Langford makes clear:

> we are invaded people, and have been since 1788 . . . We have always had to conform to the laws and standards of the invaders. Our tribal laws mean nothing to the white man, our traditional people were

classified as heathens and vermin to be cleared off the face of the earth. Assimilate us or wipe us out was the order of the day. (Langford, 1994d: 51–2)

In this age when people are becoming aware of the human rights of Aboriginal people and minority people (that is, people who, because of their small number or their limited status and power, are subordinate to a dominant culture) many Australians, both Aboriginal and non-Aboriginal, are re-examining the past in order to incorporate the histories of Aboriginal and minority people into contemporary Australian culture.

Aboriginality

Dispossessed and forced to endure the status of people systematically categorised as 'biologically inferior', Aboriginal people have until recently had limited ability to influence the writing of Australian history and to articulate their own version of that history. The Aboriginal version of how Australia was settled (or invaded) has been invisible in the sense that it has not been public knowledge; it has not been included in history books. Yet Aboriginal culture is now emerging in ways that are rewriting the history of this country. The stories that have been invisible since 1788 are appearing in print, for example in the form of Aboriginal women's life stories, which speak of the role of Aboriginal people in the formation of rural industries and the survival of Aboriginal culture into the twenty-first century.

Aboriginal people became more visible in the 1960s when they organised campaigns to improve their living conditions, to regain their traditional lands and, most prominently, to be included in the census. Before 1967 Aboriginal people were subject to special legislation and did not have full citizenship rights. In that year the Prime Minister, Harold Holt, agreed to hold a referendum to see whether white Australians would agree to amending the Constitution to allow Aboriginal people to be included in the census and to be governed by the Commonwealth (instead of the states). In the 1967 referendum about ninety percent of the Australian population agreed to the constitutional

Introduction

amendment, and for the first time Aboriginal people were governed by the same legislation as other Australians. Further activism of Aboriginal people in the 1970s led to the establishment of Aboriginal legal, health, media and education services, as well as some success with land-rights claims. Aboriginal activism has continued since then to advocate for Aboriginal people's human rights. Jackie Huggins states that 'of all the protest movements in Australia, that for Aboriginal rights has been the most persistent and widespread' (Huggins, 1991: 162).

In the 1960s Aboriginal people developed a sense of common interest and group solidarity; people from different regions over the country got together to work for reform, and the notion of a pan-Aboriginality – that is, of the common political purpose of Aboriginal people – was consolidated. Later the term 'Aboriginality' was used to describe Aboriginal people's collective identity. It provides an effective counter-discourse to the dominant white discourse which represents Aboriginal culture as lacking or inferior.

Aboriginality allows for the construction of autonomous Aboriginal identities which talk or write back to the colonising discourses which have named and defined Aboriginal people. As Daylight and Johnstone suggest, Aboriginal people are possibly the most researched demographic group in Australia (Daylight and Johnstone, 1986: 1). They have been described and defined by dominant white discourses such as that of science and anthropology (for example, the concept of evolution, which constructed Aboriginal people as more primitive than white people), that of law (which governed them as wards of the state rather than citizens with rights equal to those of white Australians) and that of religion (such as Christianity, which constructed Aboriginal people as heathen or pagan). Non-Indigenous lexicons for describing and defining Aboriginal people have proliferated; Marcia Langton (quoting John McCorquodale), for example, tells us that there have been sixty-seven definitions of Aboriginal people in Australian law (Langton, 1994: 96).

The discourse of Aboriginality thus has an important role in the rewriting of Australian history from an Aboriginal point of view and in the articulation of Aboriginal people's culture and political goals. As Ruby Langford has remarked on a number of occasions, it is important that Aboriginal people define themselves and speak for themselves (for example, see Illing, 1994: 1–2). Concepts of Aboriginality also allow Aboriginal people to develop self-determined political and cultural agendas.

Aboriginal political and cultural identities are diverse and they should not become fixed and stereotyped, nor should they be understood as static. John Fielder argues that we should read notions of Aboriginality as tactical (Fielder, 1991), Aboriginal people's own constructions of identity counteracting, for example, racist images in the media. Aboriginal constructions of contemporary Aboriginal culture and identity often draw upon the past in order to reconfigure hegemonic narratives. They create an alternative space for themselves within majoritarian culture and they affirm the continuity and persistence of Aboriginal culture. Aboriginal people's narrativisation of the past is always relative to their position in the present, and this relationship is in a constant state of flux as the present changes.

Aboriginality is thus formulated in terms of past Aboriginal culture and also in terms of Aboriginal people's current placement in majoritarian Australian and transnational contexts. Aboriginality can be said to emerge in part from the intersubjective relationship between black and white Australians, as Marcia Langton reminds us (Langton, 1994: 98–9). Before the invasion there was no Aboriginality in today's sense. Romaine Moreton, for example, says 'I see the word "Aborigine" in this country as a way of marking the beginning of colonial time' (Brewster, 2015: 59). Aboriginal people's mental geopolitical map was one of regional and 'tribal' boundaries rather than of white national borders. The presence of a dominant white culture has brought Aboriginal people together under the sign of Aboriginality with a common goal of maintaining their culture and addressing issues of dispossession and disadvantage. Because the intercultural relationship between white and black Australians is in a constant state of flux, the meaning and the goals of Aboriginality will continue to change. Concepts of Aboriginality, therefore, should be understood as contingent; they will undergo changes in response to specific political contexts and agendas.

Introduction

Nationalism

As the formerly invisible histories of Indigenous people have become visible and public, and the history and structures of colonisation continue to be exposed by the narratives of Aboriginal people, there has been a transformation in the way non-Aboriginal Australians think about both the past and the representation of the nation. Aboriginal literature puts white identity and belonging into crisis by radically problematising concepts of 'discovery', 'settlement' and 'sovereignty'. It underlines the fact that Australia was not in fact a *terra nullius* that was 'discovered' by Europeans; it had been inhabited by Aboriginal people for at least 40,000 years. Nor was the land in fact 'settled' by the invaders; the traditional hunting grounds of Aboriginal people were not relinquished willingly but were seized by force and coercion. As the original people to inhabit this land, Aboriginal people are neither settlers nor immigrants; their status as the First Australians problematises the notion of white sovereignty and white foundational narratives of nation. In the USA, the various tribes of American Indians are recognised as nations in their own right. If Indigenous sovereignty were established in Australia we would have to radically rethink majoritarian notions of the nation and investigate ethical modes of non-Indigenous belonging and cohabitation.

By taking the voices of Aboriginal writers and storytellers into account white Australians can readjust their narrative of the history of this country and imaginatively redraw their maps of Australian nationalism. Linda Burney (1994: 22–3) suggests that some of the values and practices of Aboriginal people that might contribute to a rethinking of the notion of the Australian nation are:

- **the Aboriginal concept of belonging to the land**, caring for the land, thinking in terms of 'the land our mother'.
- **the regional identity of Aboriginal people**. Aboriginal people belong to the land of Australia but first they belong to their particular country/region and language-group. It is important that we are cognisant of the regional identity of various Aboriginal writers and their membership of Indigenous nations. (Western Australian Nyoongah Rosemary van den Berg, for example, objects to being called a 'Koori' (van den Berg, 1995: 9), the name of an Eastern states

Aboriginal group.) Nyoongah writer Kim Scott talks about the recognition of regional collective identities (or Aboriginal nations) as providing a possible way forward for non-Indigenous Australians to rethink the 'shimmering' and unstable concept of the white nation (Scott, 2011).
- **the Aboriginal sense of community and interdependence**, that is, the importance of the community and the extended family.

We can identify these three key features that Linda Burney proposes in many Aboriginal women's life stories. Because their history has not until the late twentieth century been written down, in recreating their version of the colonisation of the country the early generation of Aboriginal writers drew on their memories. Deborah Bird Rose describes Aboriginal remembrance as the *'living* experience of the past, regenerated through stories' which sustain relationships with it (Rose, 1992: 15); 'as long as the conditions of the past are the conditions of the present,' she says, 'then the past is not past' (Rose, 1992: 17). She suggests that, to live in 'the richness of the present', Aboriginal people need to engage actively with their past, even though this means to 'assent to the necessity of loss' (ibid).

Jackie Huggins, an Aboriginal activist and writer, remarks upon Aboriginal people's different awareness of the past: 'Aboriginal writers', she says, 'have a stronger sense of history than their white counterparts' (Huggins, 1993: 62). Arthur Corunna, Sally Morgan's great-uncle, puts it another way: 'the black man's got a long memory,' he says (Morgan, 1987: 210). Peter Burke illuminates further the different relationships that minority (i.e. Aboriginal) and dominant (i.e. white) cultures have with the past:

> It is often said that history is written by the victors. It might also be said that history is forgotten by the victors. They can afford to forget, while the losers are unable to accept what happened and are condemned to brood over it, relive it, and reflect how different it might have been. (Burke, 1989: 106)

While it would not be appropriate to describe Aboriginal people as 'losers' (because their culture is rich, resilient and thriving in many ways), they have been subject to many forms of violence since the arrival of white people on their lands. For Aboriginal people, therefore, memory has a political and cultural significance different from that of settlers and immigrants. In many cases they are still deprived of their land and forced to endure the status of people systematically categorised as culturally 'inferior'. There has been limited recognition of Aboriginal people's contribution to the development of modern Australia. However, Aboriginal people sustain the memory of the rarely acknowledged history of labour which, as Aboriginal women attest in their life stories, had a foundational role in the development of the Australian pastoral and pearling industries. Much of this labour was exacted under exploitative conditions and some Aboriginal people have described work conditions as being those of slavery (e.g. Nannup, 1992: 52, 143; Fesl, 1993: 340; Huggins and Huggins, 1994: 39). Daisy Corunna, for example, reflects at the end of her life that she has 'been treated rotten ... like a beast of the field' and her granddaughter, Sally Morgan, sums up this life as one of being 'a work animal, nothing more' (Morgan, 1987: 352). Alice Nannup also talks at length about how she worked from the age of twelve as a domestic servant and farmhand, often without payment.

Aboriginal cultural memory preserves the unwritten black history of colonisation, which has been emerging in the public arena in the life stories of Aboriginal women. Aboriginal memory is transforming public perceptions of the past in post-invasion Australia. This memory proves to us that Aboriginal people were not simply the passive onlookers of modernisation, but rather the producers and makers of modern Australia through their labour and the knowledge of the country that they shared with the white 'settlers'.

Aboriginal Women's Life Stories

One of the predominant genres that followed the renaissance of Aboriginal literature in the 1960s and 1970s is the (auto) biographical narrative or life story. The initial wave of Aboriginal life stories in the late 1950s and the 1960s focused on men. And although men have continued to produce life stories, the genre has been dominated by women, who until the late 1980s had been less prolific as playwrights and poets (two genres which dominated the cultural and political renaissance of the 1960s and 1970s). As bibliographies by Merlan (1988), Horton (1988) and Hooton (1990) reveal, a wave of women's life stories and autobiographically based narratives began in the late 1970s and gained momentum a decade later with the publication of Sally Morgan's *My Place* (1987), which rapidly became a bestseller. Representative early titles include Oodgeroo Nunukul's *Stradbroke Dreamtime* (1972), Margaret Tucker's *If Everyone Cared* (1977), Monica Clare's *Karobran: The Story of an Aboriginal Girl* (1978), Ella Simon's *Through My Eyes (1978),* Shirley Smith and Bobbi Sykes' *Mum Shirl* (1981), Ida West's *Pride Against Prejudice* (1987), Elsie Roughsey's *An Aboriginal Mother Tells of the Old and the New* (1984) and Marnie Kennedy's *Born a Half Caste* (1985).

Morgan's success focused new attention on the genre; in Langford's words, 'her book was the first to open this country up' (Langford, 1994c: 103). As such, it represented 'a significant act of intercultural brokerage' (Donaldson, 1991: 350); in other words, it gave many Australians their first meaningful picture of contemporary urban Aboriginal people. After the publication of *My Place* the genre of Aboriginal women's life stories proliferated with Glenyse Ward's *Wandering Girl* (1988) and *Unna You Fullas* (1991), Ruby Langford Ginibi's *Don't Take Your Love to Town* (1988), Della Walker and Tina Coutts' *Me and You* (1989), Ellie Gaffney's *Somebody Now* (1989), Patsy Cohen and Margaret Somerville's *Ingelba and the Five Black Matriarchs* (1990), Doris Pilkington Garimara's *Caprice: A Stockman's Daughter* (1991), Mabel Edmund's *No Regrets* (1992), Alice Nannup's *When the Pelican Laughed* (1992) and Evelyn Crawford's *Over My Tracks* (1993). In the decade after Sally Morgan's *My Place*, the visibility of Aboriginal women's life writing continued to increase with the publication of *Bringing Them Home* (1997), the Report of the HREOC National Inquiry into the Separation of Aboriginal and Torres Strait Islander Children from their Families. Numerous critics have examined the testimonial culture produced by the *Bringing Them Home* Report (Whitlock 2001, Schaffer and Smith 2004, Kennedy 2008). Whitlock argues that reading practices which see Aboriginal life stories as testimonial narratives have proliferated in the wake of both the *Bringing Them Home* Report and the 2008 Prime Ministerial Apology to the Stolen Gener-

Introduction

ations by Kevin Rudd. She argues that new witnessing publics create testimonial cycles which give Aboriginal women's life stories a continuing mobility not only within national frameworks but in transnational networks where they resonate with global and transnational histories of slavery, child removal, decolonisation, and caste and minority civil rights movements (Whitlock, 2015). Aboriginal women's projects in telling their life stories have also converged with many other social justice and political agendas at a local level. A number of books based in South Australia such as Dulcie Wilson's *The Cost of Crossing Bridges* (1998), Doris Kartinyeri's *Kick the Tin* (2000), Veronica Brodie *My Side of the Bridge* (2002) and Doreen Kartinyeri and Sue Anderson's *My Ngarrindjeri Calling* (2008) address South Australian issues including the Hindmarsh Island issue in the 1990s.

While some of the books of the first wave focused mainly (if not exclusively) on the author, the focus of Aboriginal women's life stories widened to further include biographies and transgenerational histories of the family: Sally Morgan's second book, *Wanamurraganya* (1989), is the life story of her grandfather, and even *My Place* includes the biographies or life stories of her mother, her grandmother, and her great-uncle. Ruby Langford's second and third books, *Real Deadly* (1992a) and *My Bundjalung People* (1994a), similarly widen their focus to include the extended family. Other books of this kind include Rita and Jackie Huggins' *Auntie Rita* (1994), Rosemary van den Berg's *No Options. No Choice!* (1994) and Doris Pilkington's *Follow the Rabbit-Proof Fence* (1996). In other words, Aboriginal women's life stories increasingly included biographical as well as autobiographical materials.

The blurring of the boundaries between one's own life story and that of other family members, and the fact that the former is so intricately bound up with the latter indicates that the demarcation and nomenclature of this genre is difficult. In *My Place*, Sally Morgan's telling of her own story and her search for her identity are inextricably bound up with the discovery of her mother's, grandmother's and great-uncle's stories (see Russell West, 2003, for an interesting discussion of the discovery motif). This is true of many Aboriginal writers whose exploration of the past is an arena in which they can define their own Aboriginality. Another complicating factor is the fact that many Aboriginal life stories and autobiographical narratives are the result of collaborative projects. Some twentieth-century Aboriginal women's life stories mapped a stage in the transition in contemporary Aboriginal literature from an oral to a written culture (and here I am referring specially to page-based writing). Several of these authors wrote their books, albeit with non-Aboriginal editorial intervention: examples include Sally Morgan's *My Place* (1987), Glenyse Ward's *Wandering Girl* (1988) and *Unna You Fullas* (1991), Elsie Roughsey's *An Aboriginal Mother Tells of the Old and the New* (1984), Mabel Edmund's *No Regrets* (1992), Ellie Gaffney's *Somebody Now* (1989) and Doris Pilkington's *Caprice: A Stockman's Daughter* (1991). Sometimes a collaborative writing process is acknowledged (as in early editions of *Don't Take Your Love to Town* where copyright is shared); in other instances editors are not credited with a collaborative role (as in autobiographical narratives by Oodgeroo, Sally Morgan, Glenyse Ward, Marnie Kennedy, Mabel Edmund and Ellie Gaffney). The collaborative process produced varied outcomes. Jennifer Jones (2009: 4–47) has a particularly interesting analysis of the deleterious effects on editing on Oodgeroo's *Stradbroke Dreaming*, for example.

On the other hand, a substantial number of early Aboriginal women's life stories have been narrated orally by an Aboriginal author; then they have been recorded, transcribed and edited by an interviewer. Such narratives include those of Eliza Kennedy, Shirley Smith, Della Walker, Patsy Cohen and Alice Nannup; Sally Morgan's *My Place* is partly a transcription of taped conversations with her family (Morgan, 1988). Disinclined to take on the task of writing a whole book themselves, and yet compelled to translate traditional knowledge from an oral into a written form in order to preserve it for future generations, Aboriginal oral historians and storytellers choose to collaborate with non-Indigenous scribes. Hence the collaboration of Aboriginal women with white interviewers and editors, and with mainstream presses.

The extensive body of life writing outlined above was initially the product of a particular generation, many of whom – although not all – were members of the Stolen Generations (Morgan, Langford Ginibi and van den Berg are exceptions). Much of this life writing comprised a corrective project to restore personal, familial and communal memory and remediate it as narrative. (Some of the later life stories were motivated by additional cultural and political imperatives, such as the telling of the story of Hindmarsh Island, for example – in books by Dulcie Wilson and Veronia Brodie.) As Aboriginal literature continued to develop and diversify, the following generations of Aboriginal writers continued to exhibit a strong interest in family history and life writing. Many of the writers who have published life writing more recently are the descendants of members of the Stolen Generations or of those who had lost connection with their Aboriginal kin. Many more recent life writers were not themselves removed from their parents (for example Jackie Huggins, Larissa Behrendt, Terri Janke, Dylan Coleman and Jeanine Leane). Yet life writing and family history continue to be of central concern to this generation as demonstrated by the winning entries in the David Unaipon Award, as Jeanine Leane's research indicates (Leane, 2012). Of the twenty-four works that have received the award to date, at least nine fit into the broad category of life writing (and most of these are by women writers). Moreover, this is not a trend that shows signs of winding up; three of the most recent five books fall into this category (although they combine life story with fiction) and they are all by women writers (Munkara, Coleman and Leane).

However, the genre is changing with generational context as members of the Stolen Generations become less representative of it and textual hybridisation proliferates. Carole Ferrier (1992) argues that Indigenous life stories in print have always, to some extent, been hybrid texts; indeed, many of these texts contain features of other genres such as memoir and testimonial. I would suggest that this trend towards hybridisation has become more pronounced with the newer generations of writers who are employing a broader range of literary strategies to write about family history. One strategy is collaborative polyphonic transgenerational authorship such as Huggins (see Horáková, 2011). Another is to combine family history with fiction. In the early history of Aboriginal women's life stories, life-story telling drew on fictional techniques, for example in Doris Pilkington's *Caprice, A Stockman's Daughter* (1991) and this trend is increasing, as can be seen in Anita Heiss's *Who am I? The Diary of Mary Talence* (2001), Fabienne Bayet-Charlton's *Finding Ullagundahi Island* (2002), Tara June Winch's *Swallow the Air* (2006), Terri Janke's *Butterfly Song* (2005), Larissa Behrendt's *Home* (2004) and *Legacy* (2009), Jeanine Leane's *Purple Threads* (2011), Dylan Coleman's *Mazin' Grace* (2012) and Marie Munkara's *Every Secret Thing*

(2013). Wiradjuri life-story writer, poet and scholar Jeanine Leane argues that life stories by their very nature challenge the boundaries of fact and fiction because they 'deploy . . . a combination of fact and fiction', of 'objective' and 'subjective' modes of writing (Leane, 2012: 3).

Nomenclature has always been an issue in the field of Indigenous life writing (see Haag, 2011). Since Europeans arrived in Australia there has been a proliferation of styles and forms at the intersection of Indigenous storytelling practices and Western discursive traditions where different knowledge systems engage and compete. It's impossible to devise a watertight or definitive categorisation of the many types of life stories and narratives generated at this intersection. The field is extraordinarily diverse and inevitably exceptions arise to any rule. The term 'autobiography' was widely used in the 1980s and 1990s in relation to Indigenous life writing with the intention of positioning this writing in proximity to the literary canon in order to consolidate its legitimacy as an object of scholarly and pedagogic attention. This paralleled a wider movement in the mainstream field of autobiography to establish the genre's literary credentials (with the appearance, for example, of the foundational journal *a/b: Auto/Biography Studies* in 1985 and Doireann MacDermott's groundbreaking edited collection *Autobiographical & Biographical Writing in the Commonwealth* in 1984).

Since the 1990s scholarly work has responded to the growth of Indigenous life writing, expanding its critical vocabulary; the categories 'biography' and 'autobiography' have been complemented with cognate genres such as 'autobiographical fiction', 'life writing', 'life story', 'memoir', 'testimony', 'testimonio', 'auto-ethnography', 'trauma narratives', 'autofiction', 'literary historiography' and 'life history', each with its own critical rationale and logic. In the broader field of life writing, Sidonie Smith and Julia Watson document the fissile nature of the genre, listing sixty different types (Smith and Watson, 2010: 253). There are some problems with applying the term 'autobiography' to Aboriginal life-story writing. As I argue above, in the Western tradition, autobiography has conventionally privileged the life narrative of a single individual, often not situating them within the family or even the constitutive social networks which have shaped their subjectivity. By contrast, Indigenous authors such as Sally Morgan and Rita Huggins have produced polyphonic texts with family members that demonstrate how the individual

Introduction

is embedded in kinship relations. Secondly, many Indigenous life stories are the product of the collaborative labour of storytellers, transcribers and editors, a multiply inflected process unacknowledged by the term 'autobiography'. Thirdly, the term's emphasis on writing is in danger of obscuring the oral dimension of some stories, especially those by members of the earlier generations, who narrated them to amanuenses, editors and transcribers. In this book, therefore, I am using the term 'life story' in preference to 'autobiography'. The term 'life story', which has been in circulation since the 1980s, is a more capacious term not so narrowly delimited as 'autobiography'. It accommodates the textual hybridity of the field that draws on the techniques of fiction and historiography as well as biography and autobiography, and obviates some of the shortcomings listed above of the category of autobiography. An alternative to 'life writing' is the term 'life-history writing' (Leane, 2012) which Wiradjuri scholar Jeanine Leane uses, borrowing from Linda Westphalen (2012).

The Family as a Site of Resistance

One reason for the burgeoning of women's life stories may have been a change in the structure of Aboriginal society. Due to factors such as the disintegration of traditional family and kinship structures, alcoholism and the high incidence of Aboriginal men in jail, in recent generations women have come to occupy a prominent role in communal and family life. Black women such as Roberta Sykes have discussed the role of Aboriginal women:

> one in four black males will be dead by the age of thirty, and two of the remaining three will be incarcerated or caught up in the justice system. This means that . . . at least three out of every four black women will sleep alone, will bring up children without the benefit of black paternal presence, and will have no black male with whom to share their lives. (Sykes, 1984: 67)

Aboriginal storyteller, Patsy Cohen, explains the rise to power of women thus:

> I think after the contact with white people came in and destroyed the cultural kinship system and the way that blackfellers lived, they upset everything. They stripped the men of all their pride and respect and I think it was these, the likes of these old matriarchs, that sort of kept the men goin'. They were really strong for the men, these old women, 'cause just imagine in them times the hardship and the pressure that's put on them. (Cohen and Somerville, 1990: 109)

More recently Sally Morgan has said:

> In a lot of Aboriginal families, actually, the women are very strong. In many families I know they carry the weight of the family . . . in most Aboriginal families there is always at least one strong female character with a grandma or an auntie or somebody like that who holds everything together. (Morgan, 1992: 7, 19)

And Shirley Smith (also known as Colleen Perry) says:

> In the black world, years ago, it was a man's world. When I was running around here, thirty years ago, there wasn't too many black women going to jails and talking to every Tom, Dick and Harry or running to court or going looking in pubs for different people and drinking. They was all home. Because it was a man's world. But now, the men have got no responsibility. They've shifted everything on to the woman. Now when a man comes home, his wife is out working. Some of them get better money than the men. Black women are running things, saying things. Was a time when they'd be home having babies and saying nothing. (Smith, 1977: 249)

Women, then, over the decades, have come to occupy a focal position in Aboriginal communal and family life. The importance of family in Aboriginal women's lives and stories can be seen to run against the grain of some thinking in second-wave First World feminism which saw the family as oppressive for women. However, in the 1980s a number of Indigenous and minority women theorists critiqued second-wave white feminism. For example, black feminists from the UK and the USA argued that the family often has a different significance for minority people. Hazel Carby, for example, suggested that in the UK 'the black family has been a site of political and cultural resistance to racism' (Carby, 1982: 214); Valerie Amos and Pratibha Parmar in their work reclaimed the notion of family from white feminists and anthropologists to 'locate the Black family more firmly in the historical experiences of Black people' (Amos and Parmar, 1984: 11); and Bev Fisher argued the family is 'the last barricade between minority and lower-class people and the oppression of the state ... [and is] a shelter for the abuses of a classist, racist, sexist society' (Fisher, 1977: 13).

It is important not to idealise the family and to keep in mind, for example, that the home can also be the site of the abuse of Aboriginal women and children. Nonetheless, in their life stories many Aboriginal women describe how the family can be a site of resistance to a dominant culture which, both indirectly and directly, applies pressure to Aboriginal and minority cultures to conform and assimilate to the dominant culture's codes and conventions. As several Aboriginal women life-story authors such as Sally Morgan, Ruby Langford and Alice Nannup describe, the transgenerational memory of the impact of the Aborigines Protection Acts on Aboriginal families of the last three generations is still very strong. These Acts were introduced in the late nineteenth century, first in Victoria and then in Queensland, and in all other states (except Tasmania) in the first decade of the twentieth century. They brought in a series of regulations that subjected Aboriginal people to governmental surveillance and control in almost all aspects of their lives, and in effect segregated them from white society. They brought about the relocation of Aboriginal people into reserves or missions. Here, their travel, whom they associated with, whom they married, whom they might work for, what property they acquired and their family life were strictly monitored and supervised.

The Aborigines Protection Acts also allowed government officials to remove Aboriginal children of mixed heritage from their families and place them either in white institutions such as the missions, reserves or children's homes, or else in the employment of white people. The memory of these Acts and the way they affected many families persist for Aboriginal people. Alice Nannup describes at length her life in the Moore River Mission in Western Australia (Nannup, 1987: 96, 103, 142, 313), and we see the suspicion of authority figures and government institutions, for example, in Sally Morgan's family, particularly in her mother's and grandmother's lives and in Ruby Langford's father, who takes his family away from the Box Ridge Mission in New South Wales and later will not allow the Aborigines Protection Board to fund his daughter to go to college (Langford, 1988: 37).

The family, because it is a woman-centred arena, is a site of women's knowledge and practices. In discussing life stories by Aboriginal women, what I would like to examine is how they articulate both race and gender. On the question of race, I would like to examine how these narratives articulate a counter-narrative of Indigenous cultural memory which challenges majoritarian representations of Aboriginal people and of colonial history.

In *Domesticating Resistance* Barry Morris outlines the pervasive and entrenched network of power that has enveloped Aboriginal people since the arrival of white people in this land. This network of power is instituted and maintained by governmental regulations which involve, in Morris' words, 'a constant process of monitoring and surveillance' of the Aboriginal population (Morris, 1989: 3). In attempting to assimilate Aboriginal people to white culture, governmental policies aim to define Aboriginal identity. Aboriginal resistance to this coercion, Morris argues, is not always (although of course it can be) direct or violent. For the most part it is discrete and indirect (Morris, 1989: 4). Resistance, Morris says, refers to:

> the indirect ways in which oppressed groups gain some degree of relative autonomy by limiting or frustrating the controls those in authority exercise over their lives. Such resistances are defensive strategies which do not change the relations of oppression but contain them and remain contained by them. (Morris, 1989: 4)

So where official and unofficial networks of power attempt to dissipate and dissolve Aboriginal cultural practices by breaking down patterns of 'collective activity and associated forms of collective identity', Morris suggests that there is resistance to these pressures to fragment communities and to 'produce new forms of social individuality'. This resistance is manifested in social practices which develop a ' "way of life" in opposition to the specific structures of domination' (Morris, 1989: 4).

Introduction

In other words, in maintaining a distinct way of life Aboriginal families and communities resist the pressure to conform to a majoritarian culture. We can call this process 'developing a politics of identity', which is a phrase that Morris and many other theorists who discuss Indigenous people and minority groups use. This process is not always conscious and planned, nor is it necessarily directly or openly stated. For Aboriginal people it often takes the form of 'sustaining cultural distance from the dominant society which seeks their incorporation'(ibid). I argue, with relation to Aboriginal women's life stories, that the family is often this site of resistance and it is a site characterised by gendered knowledge. In examining Aboriginal women's life stories we can discover how this resistance is encoded within family histories.

1
Aboriginality and Sally Morgan's *My Place*

In the years following the publication of *My Place* in 1987, Sally Morgan's authenticity was challenged by a number of critics (for example, Mudrooroo 1990, Muecke 1992, Michaels 1988, Attwood 1992, Tarrago 1992 and Huggins 1993). Morgan reports that she has 'been accused of jumping on the Aboriginal bandwagon' (Graham, 1989: 58); Mudrooroo (Colin Johnson), for example, has notoriously said with reference to Morgan that 'it is considered ok to be Aboriginal as long as you are young, gifted and not very black' (Mudrooroo Narogin, 1990: 149). Other charges were that *My Place* articulates a 'bourgeois individualism' and 'an acceptance of middleclass values' (Attwood, 1992: 307, 313). Morgan's work has been compared to that of 'traditional Aboriginal genres' and found to be lacking in authenticity; her spirituality is similarly found to be impure and inauthentic because it is 'filtered' through Christianity and resembles 'New Age astrology' (Michaels, 1988: 5). Huggins has criticised *My Place* by saying that 'Aboriginality cannot be acquired overnight' (Huggins, 1993: 461).

At the heart of many of these criticisms of Sally Morgan is a suspicion over the instant and enormous success of the book. Muecke explores why white Australians have at this point in time become eager to read Aboriginal texts, and Huggins criticises the widespread use of *My Place* as the representative text of Aboriginality and as 'the only Black text on the reading list' (Huggins, 1993: 463). There is no doubt that *My Place* achieved a popular success which arguably has not been matched by another Aboriginal literary text. It has to date sold over 500,000 copies, making it one of the bestselling books in Australian literary history. There have been thirty-eight editions and it has been translated into thirteen different languages (Whitlock, 2015: 137). What I want to discuss in this chapter, however, is not so much the reception and reading of *My Place* as the general issue of Morgan's Aboriginality, focusing in particular on her relationship with the past.

I would like to reiterate the point that the concept of identity politics does not have to rely on a fixed, reified notion of identity. Rather, identity can be understood as a shifting, changing and relational thing; it is contingent and constituted according to historical and bodily circumstance and political strategy. I want to emphasise what Ruby Langford and many other Aboriginal people have said, that Aboriginal people 'should be the only ones who are responsible for defining ourselves' (Langford, 1994a: 108). My aim here is not to define Aboriginal people or Aboriginality; what I want to do is re-examine the issue of Aboriginality in relation to Sally Morgan in light of challenges to her 'authenticity' and to identify the sites at which Morgan claims difference.

The metaphors of the search and the journey suggest that Aboriginality for some people is a continuing process of negotiation and redefinition. Aboriginal writer Darlene Oxenham, for example, has written: 'reflecting on my life to date, I would summarise it as a journey towards becoming actualised as an Aboriginal' (Dudgeon et al., 1995: 18), suggesting that being Aboriginal is a process of growth and change. She also emphasises the importance of recognising that diversity exists among Aboriginal people (Dudgeon et al., 1995: 23). Marcia Langton talks about Aboriginality in terms of the relationship between black and white Australians; this relationship is constantly being renegotiated as are the concepts of Aboriginality and whiteness. The relationship between Aboriginal and non-Aboriginal Australians changes as government policies change and thus redefine it; this relationship was defined in terms of segregation in the first few decades of the twentieth century, then in terms of assimilation from the late 1930s through to the mid-1960s, of integration in the late 1960s, of self-determination from the early 1970s and Reconciliation in the 1990s. As the relationship between Aboriginal and non-Aboriginal Australians changes, so does the nature of Aboriginality, that is, the way Aboriginal people define themselves. Aboriginality is a strategic political concept. As many Aboriginal writers have said, Aboriginal people's lives are inherently political (see, for example, Romaine Moreton in Brewster, 2015: 67). Darlene Oxenham also says: 'being Aboriginal means accepting that many components of everyday life take on a political meaning' (Dudgeon et al., 1995: 20), implying that the process of defining oneself as an Aboriginal is often a political one.

If we think then of Aboriginality as a process or a journey, that journey can have different stages of realisation or 'actualisation', as Oxenham puts it. For Oxenham the experience of becoming 'actualised' as an Aboriginal and 'politicised as an individual' happened during her time at university. This process took place for Sally Morgan and her mother during their visit to their relatives in the Pilbara region of the north of Western Australia, a visit that Morgan describes as 'a spiritual and emotional pilgrimage' (Morgan, 1987: 233). It was a period of transformation for Morgan: 'we were different people . . . we had an Aboriginal consciousness' (Morgan, 1987: 233). This visit proved to be a revelation and a turning point for Morgan and her family; it affirmed their Aboriginality after a long period of denial. Peter Read, in the introduction to the book he edited with Coral Edwards called *The Lost Children* (1989), which is a collection of stories from people who had been removed as children from their Aboriginal parents as a result of the Aborigines Protection Act and placed in white families, suggests that even after a white upbringing many of these people later in life identified as Aboriginal (after all, being removed gave these people a different history to other Australians who were not removed); 'Aboriginal identity is recoverable', Read suggests (Read, 1989: xvii).

Daisy Corunna and Gladys Milroy

Their Aboriginality had by no means been a constant thing for Sally, her mother or her grandmother; indeed, they all had at one time or another an ambivalent attitude towards identifying as Aboriginal. If Sally had no knowledge of her Aboriginality until her late childhood, she is a representative of but one generation in a genealogy of child removal that extends through her mother and her grandmother. (For example, through the WA *Aborigines Act* of 1905, both Daisy Corunna and later Gladys Milroy were removed from their Aboriginal mothers. Daisy was brought up in a white family, and Gladys in a children's home.) It is in fact impossible to talk about Sally's Aboriginality without reference to the impact of child removal policies on her mother and grandmother.

My Place is a testimony to the effects of the assimilation policy, introduced in the late 1930s, which attempted to bring about the absorption of Aboriginal people into white society, thereby erasing their cultural difference (and, it might be argued, the memory of the aggressivity and violence of colonisation). The assimilation policy held sway until the 1960s when Aboriginal groups and their supporters challenged the idea that Aboriginal people should give up their identity in order to assimilate to white culture. *My Place* shows how, during the 1940s and 1950s, both Daisy and Gladys felt ashamed and fearful of identifying as Aboriginal. They denied their Aboriginality and attempted to repress their memories of the past.

My Place is the story of the excavation of the family's history by a younger woman for whom Aboriginality became a badge of pride rather than of shame or fear. It tells of Morgan's excitement over her newfound heritage and also her frustration in trying to unlock the secrets of the family's painful and humiliating past. Her reaction to her family's complicity with the assimilationist era is one of frustration, sadness and anger. The book is a story of the dislocation of generations; where her grandmother and mother had hidden their past and their Aboriginality, Morgan wanted to reclaim and make visible the past, an action fiercely resisted by her grandmother. Morgan and her grandmother grew up in very different historical circumstances and this difference generates the narrative tension of the book. The absurdity and pathos and, as some Aboriginal commentators have suggested, the shame of denying their Aboriginality are well illustrated in the family's story, which thus reveals the devastating effects of racism on Aboriginal people's identity.

In examining the attitudes of Gladys Milroy and Daisy Corunna towards their Aboriginality, we see that they both eschew or refuse the name 'Aboriginal' at various times in their lives. Daisy admits that she 'wanted to be white' (Morgan, 1987: 336) and Gladys says of her

1 Aboriginality: Sally Morgan

that 'she just doesn't want to be Aboriginal' (Morgan, 1987: 229). Her brother, Arthur Corunna, explains her denial of her Aboriginality as the result of a feeling of shame (Morgan, 1987: 148). Even when Daisy does admit to her brother that 'I may be a blackfella', she qualifies this with the significant statement: 'but I'm not like you. I dress decent and I know the right way to do things' (Morgan, 1987: 147). It seems that she is differentiating her Aboriginality from a working-class Aboriginality. But even though *My Place* bears witness to the women's ambivalent relationship with their Aboriginality, the book often paints a satirical picture of whiteness. There are many funny incidents where Daisy's narrative voice describes the absurdity and strangeness of English middle-class etiquette and such things as building a tennis court in the bush (Morgan, 1987: 327), mimicking an English nanny (Morgan, 1987: 333), ironing bed sheets (Morgan, 1987: 334) and cutting the crusts off sandwiches (Morgan, 1987: 334). 'Funny, isn't it?' she says, inviting the reader to view these rituals through the ironic gaze of an Aboriginal woman.

We see, for example, how odd the ritual of formal morning and afternoon teas must have appeared to her, transplanted as they were from the context of upper-class English life to that of colonial, suburban Australia and Indigenous people who had no idea of the original context and significance of English etiquette. It is only when Daisy sees this ritual enacted in an English film on TV that she recognises the role that she had been trained to play; that is, she recognises herself for the first time as a servant defined by a specific class etiquette:

> I 'member they used to have real fancy morning and afternoon teas. The family would sit on the lawn under a big, shady umbrella. I'd bring out the food and serve them. You know, I saw a picture like that on television. It was in England, they were all sittin' outside in their fancy clothes with servants waitin' on them. I thought, well fancy that, that's what I used to do. They must have that silly business in quite a few countries. (Morgan, 1987: 334–5)

The humour of the passage derives from the fact that the formal occasions of morning and afternoon tea are defamiliarised when we view them through Daisy Corunna's eyes. From her point of view we see the absurdity of the occasion with its formal pomp and frills, the 'fancy clothes' of the upper class. Through her eyes we see these formal occasions as 'silly business'. It is significant that this ritual only makes sense to Daisy Corunna when she sees it many years later on TV. At that point she recognises the class origin and context of the ritual, namely 'England'. In reading about Daisy's reaction the readers themselves can see the comic strangeness of transplanting a culture from one context into an entirely different context.

In *My Place* we see that for much of her life Daisy Corunna had attempted to repress her Aboriginality. She refers to Aboriginal people as 'them' (e.g. Morgan, 1987: 144) and states that she wanted to be white (Morgan, 1987: 336). Morgan describes Daisy's attempt to identify as white during the visit by the rent man when he and Daisy are talking about how wonderful God was in creating nature. Daisy is using this opportunity to impress the rent man, whose power she has always feared, believing that he might one day evict them or cause the government to intervene in other ways in their lives. While rhapsodising over the wonder of God in making the earth's creatures she says, 'here are you and I, both white, and we couldn't do that' (Morgan, 1987: 107). At first for Sally, overhearing this event is ludicrously funny, but then she is overcome with sadness and asks herself:

> why did she want to be white? Did she really equate being white with the power of God, or was it just a slip of the tongue? I realised, with sudden insight, that there must have been times in her life when she'd looked around and the evidence was right before her eyes. If you're white, you can do anything. (Morgan, 1987: 107)

Like Sally, we realise that Nan's apparently absurd effort to deny her Aboriginality and to mimic being white reveals a profound sense of powerlessness. If white people in Daisy's eyes had a power that could be compared to God's, as Sally suggests, Daisy's experience of being Aboriginal was one comparable to that of being one of God's creatures, that is, of being totally controlled by him and subject to his law and his power. The reader, like Sally, is aware of the pathos of Daisy's need to mask her Aboriginality.

1 Aboriginality: Sally Morgan

Despite the fact that on occasions like these Daisy Corunna demonstrated the desire to mask or conceal her Aboriginality, we can detect a deep-seated ambivalence in her, for at other times she affirms her blackness. We are told that on occasion she not only identifies as a Nyoongah (an Aboriginal woman from South-West Australia), having seen Nyoongahs on TV, but she identifies with all other black people as well (Morgan, 1987: 138); as the narrator puts it, 'in a sense they were her people, because they shared the common bond of blackness and the oppression that, for so long, that colour had brought' (Morgan, 1987: 138). Perhaps her ambivalence about her Aboriginality and this confusion of roles and identities is best summed up by Daisy herself: 'There I was, stuck in the middle. Too black for the whites and too white for the blacks' (Morgan, 1987: 336).

Gladys Milroy also inhabits a complex and ambivalent identity. For her, identity, as for her mother, was a matter of acting out roles and mimicking white people and a white way of life. In order to disguise her Aboriginality she had been 'inventing stories and making exaggerated claims since the day she was born' (Morgan, 1987: 137). One such story was the tale she told her children, that 'Nan had come out on a boat from India in the early days' (Morgan, 1987: 99). When Sally confronts her with concealing the family's Aboriginality, she attempts to defend herself: 'it was only a little white lie' (Morgan, 1987: 135). The (unintended) irony of this phrase is resounding. Later, however, when she meets her relatives in the Pilbara, Gladys acknowledges the heritage she has denied herself: 'All my life, I've only been half a person' (Morgan, 1987: 233).

Sally herself follows a similar trajectory. At first she has a great deal of trouble believing or accepting that the family is Aboriginal (e.g. Morgan, 1987: 105). When she does decide to identify as Aboriginal she discovers that it is a confusing process; 'what did it really mean to be Aboriginal?' she asks herself (Morgan, 1987: 141). Her point of reference is always her grandmother; 'if she wasn't white, then neither were we' (Morgan, 1987: 97) she reasons, and 'my grandmother's Aboriginal and it's a part of me, too' (Morgan, 1987: 137). Later she says, 'if I denied my tentative identification with the past now, I'd be denying her as well' (Morgan, 1987: 141).

The Past

As this last passage suggests, Sally's connection with her grandmother is the point at which she affirms her Aboriginality. Just as Ruby Langford opens her second book, *My Bundjalung People,* with the sentence 'I wanted to travel back to the country where I was born to find my roots,' (Langford, 1994a) so *My Place* is a quest narrative where the narrator is in search of the familial past. Not only has the history of the colonisation of Aboriginal people been suppressed from white histories, but we can see how it is also suppressed or forgotten within some Aboriginal families.

The erasure of memories in Sally Morgan's family had been effected for the purposes of some measure of assimilation. In rejecting assimilation and the subordination of Aboriginal people and culture Morgan delves into the past, into the stories of her mother, her grandmother and her great-uncle (and, in her second book, *Wanamurraganya,* the stories of her grandfather), in order to reclaim a 'place' for her Aboriginality in the contemporary world. In writing the history of her family, she is reclaiming the past from the obliteration that the assimilation policies brought. By collecting and writing down the memories of her family she is in effect reorganising the memory of the family in a way that creates new knowledge. This knowledge is both private and public; the violence and brutality of the colonial encounter is reinscribed in the family history and in the wider collective memory and history of the nation.

Andrew Lattas suggests that reclaiming and recreating the past is a way of 'formulating an uncolonised space to inhabit', 'an alternative space from which to reflect upon the terms of present existence' (Lattas, 1993: 254). He points to the 'need to create new mythic narratives for regaining and healing the lost side of one's being' (Lattas, 1993: 257). For Morgan this mythic narrative is the narrative of the family, both her immediate suburban family and her extended family in the Pilbara. The family is a complex system both of storytelling and of silences. It is a site of spiritual as well as bodily connections and 'belongings', of the 'black blood' that links Morgan with the past.

1 Aboriginality: Sally Morgan

The Family and Storytelling

I have suggested that the family is a focal point of difference for Sally Morgan. She frequently contrasts her family with those of her school friends, for example. Not only did they appear different, a difference that they initially put down to being Indian (Morgan, 1987: 38), but the atmosphere and the relationships in their family were different from those in the families of her school friends. She observes that the bond between her and her siblings seems stronger than that in other families: 'we felt our family was the most important thing in the world', she says (Morgan, 1987: 38). The Milroy family is characterised further by 'tall stories and jokes' (Morgan, 1987: 84). It is the site of storytelling, an important means by which Aboriginality is constructed and transmitted. Storytelling is the means by which memory is passed on from one generation to the next and the family history preserved. Memory and storytelling are especially important in oral communities where there is no other way of preserving history, and we know that Daisy Corunna was not able to read or write. Like many Aboriginal children taken away from their families, she believed that she was going to get an education; in this matter, like many other Aboriginal people, she was sadly disappointed (Morgan, 1987: 333).

Thus the family is the locus of storytelling for Morgan and for many other contemporary Aboriginal women, as their life stories demonstrate. We can clearly see the marks of storytelling in the narrative of *My Place*. The majority of Sally's anecdotes in the book are told about the family and, presumably, *to* the family on different occasions. Each of the early chapters, for example, is a series of small incidents, most of which are humorous. The butt of many jokes is a source of authority, be it the school, religion or a formal occasion (as when the family has a visit from a Legatee [Morgan, 1987: 93]); in the latter case the joke is on the outsider and affirms the family's strength and togetherness, but more often than not the joke is at a family member's expense. Laughter is a means of relieving tension and stress, of coping with difficulty and anger. Anger is often diffused by laughter, for example in the incident where Sally is teasing her sister about the devil's finger (Morgan, 1987: 63).

In a similar episode Morgan speaks about her mother's interest in religion with a great deal of humour. She describes her mother's religious faith as a 'secret weapon' which she hoped would aid in controlling her children. Morgan describes how her mother 'wasn't biased when it came to religion. We attended the Roman Catholic, Baptist, Anglican, Church of Christ and Seventh Day Adventist churches' (Morgan, 1987: 62). However, the seriousness of conventional religion didn't impress Sally much as a child. She gently parodies the ineffectiveness of systems of control and implies that children have a playfulness and irreverence that expose the conventions of authority, which adults take so seriously.

Even the awe-inspiring figure of the devil, which supposedly impressed upon children the severity of evil, loses its convincing aura of power due to various technical mishaps during the showing of a film:

> This time, the devil appeared. He was predominantly black, except for a red face, and two small, red horns. His long, dark cape billowed around him like a bulging thunder-cloud. Lightning flashed, sharp and yellow, across the screen, illuminating his awesome visage. The rain clouds above shook, heaved and burst forth, but the rain turned to hissing steam when it reached the devil, who kept shooting bright, red flames from his large pitchfork.
>
> If it hadn't been for the sound-track, we would have been terrified. He was the most frightening creature we'd ever seen. However, each time he threw back his horny red head and laughed a presumably wicked laugh, the only sound we heard was that of rushing heavenly voices singing Alleluia, Praise the Lord! (Morgan, 1987: 62–3)

The bombastic, elevated language ('the rain clouds above shook, heaved and burst forth'), and the caricatured imagery of the devil's dark cape, red horns and pitchfork, create a lively sense of comedy here. As readers we share Sally's perception of the devil as a ridiculous figure. The comic contrast between the 'awesome visage' of the devil, and the accompanying storm, and the 'heavenly voices singing Alleluia' dispels the power of the image of the devil to terrify. The child's ability to view figures of authority (in this case the religious symbol of the devil, which is intended to intimidate and warn people of the dangers of sin) as ridiculous, psychologically removes the child from the influence of this system of authority. Humour and laughter often function in this way in Aboriginal culture to parody the systems of authority that have oppressed Aboriginal people (see for example, Marie Munkara's discussion in Brewster, 2015). Additionally, humour is a means of coping with the pain and anguish of the past; we are told for example, that Gladys used humour to hide painful feelings (Morgan, 1987: 215).

Storytelling, as we see from the passage above, is an important activity in *My Place*. Arthur Corunna is keen to tell his story, not only so that his own family will know of the past, but so that white people will know the Aboriginal version of history. He takes storytelling very seriously; he emphasises the factual nature of his story and its truth. He wants to share his life story with others so that the history of Aboriginal people may be known. Indeed, he describes his story as 'history' (Morgan, 1987: 161). Gladys also takes Sally's book very seriously:

> There's been nothing written about people like us, all the history's about the white man. There's nothing about Aboriginal people and what they've been through. (Morgan, 1987: 161)

Nan also takes the truth of storytelling seriously: 'you can't put no lies in a book,' she says (Morgan, 1987: 325). This reminds us of Ruby Langford's notion of storytelling and the fact that she distinguishes her writing very sharply from fiction; she describes herself as 'a true storyteller'; 'I'm not interested in fiction,' she says (Langford, 1994c: 109). She also says that she wants to 'store all this knowledge about my mob here so that we don't get left out of the next lot of history ... because we've been locked completely out of this one' (Langford, 1994c: 108).

Storytelling thus has multiple roles. As a vehicle for maintaining and transmitting knowledge and memory it not only binds the family together by establishing their link with the past, but it also has the role of educating non-Aboriginal people as to those parts of history that have remained invisible. If storytelling is an important part of family life, so too is silence. Stephen Muecke (1992) suggests that Daisy Corunna's refusal to reveal all her 'secrets' to Sally Morgan is for her an act of resistance to the demand to speak. Aboriginal people have for a long time been interviewed by anthropologists and government officials who document and define their lives and their culture; resisting the demand to speak and reveal information can thus be seen as a way of Aboriginal people asserting ownership of their lives and their culture – in other words, of establishing their power. Ken Gelder similarly points out that many Aboriginal narratives are as much about evasion as about informing. Not only do Aboriginal people tell their history and thus act to intervene in the white discourse of history, but the refusal of their stories to tell all makes the point that 'there is always something unavailable' (Gelder, 1991: 357); the stories are as much about 'secrecy and strategic non-disclosure' (Gelder, 1991: 360) as they are about the giving of information. Wiradjuri writer Jeanine Leane talks about the importance of secrets in her family where the Aboriginal women in the family were not allowed by the white patriarch to express their Aboriginality (see Brewster, 2015).

It is at this point that we realise that these stories are not merely for non-Indigenous readers' edification and entertainment; they are not told simply for non-Indigenous people's consumption; at the very point that they resist consumption these stories reveal the existence of other knowledges, some of which will remain inaccessible to non-Aboriginal people. The revealing and imparting of knowledge is always an act of ownership, as is the keeping of secrets. In *My Place* we see a tension between two different generational reactions to the past: Sally's and her grandmother's. To some extent Sally does not understand the role secrecy has played in her grandmother's life (where secrets have possibly shielded her from shame and exposure) as she presses her grandmother for more information: 'you dunno what a secret is', her grandmother tells her (Morgan, 1987: 319). Even Arthur doesn't really understand what her 'secrets' mean to his sister; he thinks the telling of 'history' is much more important (Morgan, 1987: 165). Nan would appear to have different kinds of secrets; some relate to painful and traumatic incidents of the past, while others relate to spiritual knowledge such as her healing powers (Morgan, 1987: 346). It is significant that Nan was not the only member of Sally's family who kept the painful parts of her past a secret; Sally's father Bill had never revealed to his wife and family the most traumatic aspects of his wartime experience (Morgan, 1987: 289).

1 Aboriginality: Sally Morgan

While clearly there had been pain and disturbance in this family, particularly around the shadowy figure of Bill, the family for people such as Sally's mother and grandmother is also a site of resistance and a haven from the racism of the outside world. It is particularly important for the Milroy family, given that both Daisy and Gladys were removed from their families as children. The family for Sally is a retreat from school and from the outside world. At a time when the family was examining its own past it became like a cocoon (Morgan, 1987: 307). Both the older women suffered the anxiety that Gladys' children would be removed from them, an anxiety that was the legacy of the WA *Aborigines Act* of 1905; hence the family lived as if under siege, fearing that at any day the government might intervene, for example, when Gladys' husband Bill died (Morgan, 1987: 348). This was why Daisy and Gladys decided to conceal their Aboriginality from the children (Morgan, 1987: 305). It is also why they both remain suspicious of government institutions (such as the hospital and the housing bureau) and why they are so easily intimidated by and unable to deal with authority, difficulties that Sally shares with them (Morgan, 1987: 96, 103, 142).

The concept of 'belonging' is also very important, both in the sense of belonging to a place and to people and country. Arthur talks about going walkabout to visit his relatives, the people that 'belonged to us' (Morgan, 1987: 175), and Sally talks about the welcome her family got from their relatives in the Pilbara, which gave them 'a sense of belonging' (Morgan, 1987: 232). This feeling works two ways; the people in the Pilbara are also pleased that their light-skinned relatives who had been taken away from them wanted to 'own' them (Morgan, 1987: 228–9). It is through a clarification of their family group relationship that Morgan is able to affirm her place in her extended family; as Billy Swan tells her: 'you got your place now' (Morgan, 1987: 232). We can see that the 'place' in the title of her book refers both to her place in the Aboriginal extended family and to the place of Aboriginal people in Australia and in public memory, a place that has previously been denied them. They have been denied this both at the family level and at the societal level. For people of Daisy and Arthur's generation, for example, their sense of 'belonging' to white families was fraught because parentage was denied by white people (and this then impacted upon people such as Nan); as

Daisy says, 'that's the trouble with us blackfellas, we don't know who we belong to, no one'll own up' (Morgan, 1987: 325).

At times Daisy is let down by the white family for which she worked (and which, *My Place* implies, fathered her, despite the fact that they never acknowledged this). Gladys is distressed by this treatment of her mother and also feels let down by this family. She affirms that she did not 'belong' to the Drake-Brockman family: 'they'd treated me like one of the family in the past, but I was glad now that I didn't belong to them' (Morgan, 1987: 274). In this context the statement is one of resistance and autonomy, especially in light of the fact that when Daisy, for example, was younger she had felt they 'owned' her, much the same way as they owned their house or their car. In this sense relations between Aboriginal people and their 'employers', and the exploitation of Aboriginal labour, have often been described as slavery (see, for example, Fesl, 1993: 340; Huggins and Huggins, 1994: 39); what Daisy and Gladys are refusing here is the role of the slave.

Spirituality

The concept of belonging is occasionally expressed in the mythic imagery of genetic or bodily inheritance. Nan uses the imagery of 'black blood' to affirm Sally's connection with the family, its Aboriginality and its past: on account of Sally's 'black blood', Nan says, 'you belonged to us' (Morgan, 1987: 348). It affirms Sally's spirituality and, in particular, her link with the land: when Nan says to Sally 'you kids loved the bush, you got things passed down to you from Gladdie and me. Things that you only got 'cause we was black,' (Morgan, 1987: 348) she implies that a love of the bush is a bodily and spiritual thing and an aspect of Aboriginality that is inherited. Nan affirms this notion of inheritance when she tells Sally, 'you ... got a feel for the spiritual side of things ... you never know what's gunna get passed down' (Morgan, 1987: 348).

Many Aboriginal people see their spirituality as an emblem of Aboriginality; 'our people was strong in the spirit,' Nan says (Morgan, 1987: 348); 'blackfellas know all 'bout spirits' (Morgan, 1987: 344). It is also a marker of difference; in contrast to Aboriginal people, white people are 'only living half a life' as they don't generally have access to the spiritual world (Morgan, 1987: 344). Aboriginal spirituality takes various forms in *My Place*. One of these is a love of the bush. The swamp, in particular, is a playground for the children, as Morgan describes: 'I imagined myself as an adventurer, always curious to know what was around the next bend, or behind the clump of taller gums that I glimpsed in the distance' (Morgan, 1987: 59). The swamp and the bush also instil in the children a love of nature; Morgan describes how the swamp became 'part of me, part of what I was as a person' (Morgan, 1987: 59). From this point of view it has a spiritual significance and is a site of comfort and protection. Gladys Milroy and Daisy Corunna hear Aboriginal voices and music coming from the swamp; Gladys says 'whenever I heard it, it was like a message, like I was being supported, protected' (Morgan, 1987: 292), and Daisy also says of the voices in the swamp, 'I think now they was protectin' us' (Morgan, 1987: 347). Birds and animals are part of both the physical and the spiritual world, as we well know from the bird call that Jill hears announcing Nan's death (Morgan, 1987: 356). Spirituality is also manifested in Nan's special healing powers (Morgan, 1987: 346). Nan, Gladys and Sally each have spiritual visions and dreams, which often arise out of despair (e.g. Morgan, 1987: 227, 295, 297). We can see that this spirituality is hybrid and draws not only on visions of the past and traditional Aboriginal culture, such as the Aboriginal music from the swamp, but also on Christian imagery. For example Gladys has visions of angels (Morgan, 1987: 292) and of Christ (Morgan, 1987: 301–2) and Sally has a vision of her relatives in heaven (Morgan, 1987: 227).

Conclusion

We have seen that Aboriginality is contingent and historical. Alison Brumbie, one of the characters in Aboriginal playwright Eva Johnson's play *What Do They Call Me?* asks: 'who has the magic formula to say what makes you Aboriginal?' (Johnson, 1991: 254). There is no answer to this rhetorical question; there is no magic formula. To understand what is meant by Aboriginality, non-Aboriginal people such as myself look to Aboriginal people and the way they define their Aboriginality. And as I suggested earlier, while the concept of a pan-Aboriginality is useful in giving Aboriginal people unity and solidarity, there are many variations of the notion of Aboriginality as Aboriginal people articulate their sense of self, history and culture.

Life stories are one means of articulating these things. In *My Place* we see that Sally Morgan's sense of herself and her Aboriginality are intricately tied up with her family and in particular with her mother and grandmother and their history of racialised oppression. Her grandmother's life holds the memory of the shameful economic and sexual exploitation of Aboriginal women. Morgan turns to the past in order to retrieve the history of her family, and in articulating one Aboriginal family's painful excavation of their repressed past, illuminates aspects of racism and violence in white Australian culture that have also been repressed, in this case in a form of collective amnesia.

Deborah Bird Rose has said that there can be no equitable future without due recognition of the past and that it is the oral narratives of Aboriginal people that show us 'how to reclaim the past in order to liberate the future' (Rose, 1989: 146). It is important that non-Aboriginal Australians reacquaint themselves with their past, and not simply in order to charge each other with blame and guilt; guilt can be an excuse for non-action. Aboriginal people have emphasised the need for white Australians to move beyond their guilt, as it prevents them from developing a new understanding of Aboriginal people; Ruby Langford, for example, states: 'perhaps one day we will receive the recognition we truly deserve when white Australia overcomes all their guilty feelings about us' (Langford, 1994a: 135). Noel Pearson similarly observes that 'it is those who refuse to recognise and acknowledge the past who are most troubled by guilt. Only with acknowledgment can the debilitating baggage of our past be dispensed with' (Pearson, 1994: 3).

It is important that non-Aboriginal Australians revisit the past in order to understand Aboriginal people better and to understand the violence of colonial history and its legacies. Aboriginal people's relationship with the past is different from that of non-Aboriginal people because the two groups have very different histories. Aboriginal women life-story authors, by recording their memory and that of their families, become custodians of their familial history. Sally Morgan and her sister, for example, make a pact to bear witness to the past, to their grandmother's life and to their own Aboriginality: 'we would never forget,' they promise their grandmother (Morgan 1987: 354).

In a sense *My Place* reads like an elegy for Daisy Corunna. *My Place*, like much Aboriginal literature, is a book about loss, the loss of traditional culture as much as of individual family members, and a mourning not only of their passing but of the suffering and exploitation they endured, which has rarely been acknowledged. I talked in the Introduction about how the change in non-Aboriginal Australians' awareness of the past will result in a change in the way non-Aboriginal Australians conceive of their nation's history. A more representative understanding of the nation would be grounded in recognition and acknowledgement of the many ramifications of the violence that Indigenous people experienced in the colonial encounter, and of the continuity of contemporary Aboriginal culture.

2
Issues of Race and Gender in Ruby Langford's *Don't Take Your Love To Town*

This chapter examines issues of race and gender in Bundjalung writer Ruby Langford's life story *Don't Take Your Love to Town* (1988). I have suggested that in maintaining a distinct way of life and identity, Aboriginal families and communities resist the pressure to conform to a majoritarian white culture. The memory of the ironically named Aborigines Protection Acts, established in the early part of the twentieth century, has haunted Aboriginal families. Many people affected by these acts felt the need to keep their families together, and even where families were not broken up by the removal of children, the threat of this happening and the fear and suspicion of and bitterness towards the white authorities lingered. We see this in *Don't Take Your Love to Town* when Ruby's father will not allow the Aborigines Protection Board to send her to Teachers' College (Langford, 1988: 37).

Ruby's father took his girls out of the Box Ridge mission where they were born and they lived an itinerant lifestyle in country towns. The 'extended family' features prominently in Ruby's early life, as she often lived with relatives and friends. Later, when she had a family of her own, that family and the maintenance of it was a very important part of her life.

The Family

I will focus here on the role of the family in *Don't Take Your Love to Town* and examine Ruby Langford's family as the site of what I shall refer to as 'subjugated knowledges', that is, knowledges which, because they are not understood as scientific, are not considered authoritative. The family and its subjugated knowledges are the site of resistance to a dominant culture which attempts to manage expressions of Aboriginal identity. The life stories of Aboriginal women articulate not only how Aboriginal women have been racialised, that is, how the government policies of managing Aboriginal people impacted upon them, but they also articulate something specific about the gender of the people who have lived and narrated these stories. Aboriginal women's life stories are shaped by both gender and race.

Women and children form the hub of the family. The men in *Don't Take Your Love to Town* (from Langford's father onwards) drift in and out of the family. In addition, white men do not participate in the extended family community. When Langford is living at St George in the bush with Gordon Campbell, for example, she does not enjoy the benefits of the extended family network:

> I felt like I was living tribal but with no tribe around me, no closeknit family. The food-gathering, the laws and songs were broken up, and my generation at this time wandered around as if we were tribal but in fact living worse than the poorest of poor whites, and in the case of women living hard because it seemed like the men loved you for a while and then more kids came along and the men drank and gambled and disappeared. One day they'd had enough and they just didn't come back. It happened with Gordon and later it happened with Peter. (Langford, 1988: 96)

The white men in her life did not feel happy in the extended family environment, as we see when Peter comes to join Langford's family in Sydney and is not comfortable in the 'mob scene' of the large family living in a two-bedroom flat (Langford, 1988: 102). Langford's Aboriginal partners too, participate only spasmodically in parenting. Her first partner Sam, for example, meeting up with her again after a long absence, barely spares a thought for or even a glance at his children (Langford, 1988: 101). Men do occasionally have redeeming features when it comes to parenting, however – for example, in the humorous incident when Langford's partner Lance disciplines her boys, who had run away and been returned by the police:

> I said to Lance when we got home, 'Take them upstairs and give them a good belting'. He frog-marched them upstairs and we could hear the yells. Serves them right, we thought, they deserve it. We didn't find out for years that Lance was hitting the beds and telling them to yell like they were getting hit. They kept this secret well. (Langford, 1988: 128)

The extended family network was particularly important in the context of Langford's and other Aboriginal people's itinerant lifestyle. The family in *Don't Take Your Love to Town* moves between rural and urban districts of New South Wales, Victoria and Queensland. A mobile lifestyle such as this, occasioned as it is by availability of work and by the needs and demands of relatives, is sustained by a complex of communities. On a number of occasions Langford describes the importance of cohabitation to extended families. This, she says, is a need dictated by both economic and emotional concerns.

Tim Rowse has suggested that Langford's struggle to raise her family is indicative of the decline and disintegration of the traditional extended family and kinship network (Rowse, 1993a; 1993b). I would argue that these networks do nevertheless survive in both the rural and urban environments of *Don't Take Your Love to Town*. Langford's two following books, *Real Deadly* (1992) and *My Bundjalung People* (1994), describe further her search for her roots and her return to the places of her childhood and her ancestors, where she renews contact with family and friends; 'this world is getting smaller by the minute', she exclaims on meeting old friends in *My Bundjalung People* (Langford, 1994a: 174), a remark which attests to the strength and the survival of the bonds of family and friends.

In a society where men were often absent due to work, alcoholism or being in jail, the women had to depend on each other. There are many affirmations of women's friendships in the book, many of them humorous, such as Ruby and Neddy's friendship, which survived the stealing of each other's lovers. When Neddy had an affair with Ruby's partner Ruby didn't talk to her for four years, but eventually forgave her. As she put it much later:

> Nerida and I have been friends for about thirty-eight years of our lives, and the only time we had a row was over a man, and we didn't think it was worth losing our friendship over. (Langford, 1988: 221)

And, in fact, when Ruby had sex with Neddy's man, Neddy made a joke of the incident and Ruby relates the incident with characteristic humour:

> We got so pissed that when I woke up next morning Bob was on the divan beside me. I was embarrassed about this, he was Neddy's boyfriend. Oh well, she would take these little holidays.
> When she came back I told her about it. She had a good laugh about my embarrassment and said, 'OK, he's your boyfriend now. No problem, plenty more fish in the sea.' (Langford, 1988: 150–1)

The bonding between women is thus quite strong, especially with their common interest in children. In another humorous moment Langford describes meeting Nerida after some years and catching up on news. She says: 'Altogether she had ten kids and with my eight it took all afternoon to catch up on the news' (Langford, 1988: 127).

To be living in a community is thus very important to Langford. Langford describes living at Katoomba in the Blue Mountains in a house that someone had offered them: 'Katoomba had been a healthy life but isolated – not enough Kooris to go around' (Langford, 1988: 126); hence her decision to move back to an inner-city area. She had the same problem with the housing commission house in Green Valley, and she has some strong statements to make about the government's policy of 'integration' in the late 1960s and early 1970s, which she says meant 'splitting up the Aboriginal communities' (Langford, 1988: 176). The rule that you weren't able to have anyone stay without permission from the Commission was a re-enactment of the monitoring and surveillance of Aboriginals in the missions, Langford says; the rule violated a central aspect of Aboriginal life, namely that 'survival often depended on being able to stay with friends and relatives' (Langford, 1988: 174). Elsewhere she says, 'I always had a houseful wherever I went. It was a means of survival' (Langford, 1988: 158).

Clearly, survival for Langford and her family is quite different from survival as it understood by middle-class white Australians. She talks about survival here in an economic sense and in an emotional sense, but also in the literal sense of staying alive. The word takes on especially resonant significance towards the end of the narrative when several of the men of her extended family, such as her brother Kevin and her son Nobby, fight simply to maintain the will to survive. Kevin loses this battle and we have the feeling that Nobby is often close to losing it. Langford's other two sons, David and Jeff, also seem periodically to be fighting depression; David eventually loses this battle. We can see in these portraits the devastating personal repercussions of race and class inequality on Aboriginal men's mental and spiritual health. In some cases the challenges facing Aboriginal men are different to those facing women. Dispossession, Langford argues, 'has turned our men into people with no hope, no pride, no nothing' (Langford, 1994b: 81).

Subjugated Knowledges

I mentioned earlier that the family can be seen as the site of subjugated knowledges (Foucault, 1980: 81). Foucault argues that some kinds of knowledge, because they cannot be verified by science, are considered to be naive, unauthoritative and unimportant. They are placed low in the hierarchies of knowledge in Western society. However, these subjugated knowledges tell us a lot about the marginalised group to which they belong. They articulate knowledges that have been repressed and denied by the dominant group. One example of these subjugated knowledges in Langford's narrative is Aboriginal spirituality. *Don't Take Your Love to Town* is littered with references to a network of intuitive sensations which links family members together. The narrative opens with Langford telling us about her totem, the willy wagtail, and the special significance it has for her.

There are constant references to visitations of dead people's spirits and also to spiritual practices such as 'calling the porpoises in' by singing. Langford describes how a man explained to her why an old Aboriginal woman at Yamba used to stand on the top of the cliff and sing. As a result, 'the porpoises circled the beach all day while the people were swimming, and headed out to sea when everyone was gone. He told me there'd never been a shark attack on that beach' (Langford, 1988: 39). It is interesting that the narrator does at times express scepticism, as in this incident, but leaves it to the reader to decide: 'I didn't know whether to believe the old man or not, but the porpoises circled the beach every day we were there' (Langford, 1988: 39). In this passage Langford both expresses some hesitation over the incident ('I didn't know whether to believe the old man or not') and presents the contradicting 'evidence' of fact ('the porpoises circled the beach every day we were there'). These are two conflicting comments on the event linked by the inconclusive word 'but'; Langford conveys both belief and disbelief without making a final judgement one way or the other. The reader may be left in a state of uncertainty in the face of traditional Aboriginal practices such as this.

Clearly this knowledge is incommensurate with a Western belief system, and Langford does not try to persuade; she lets these little snippets of spiritual knowledge sit separately within the text. So we have two different systems of belief in one text. For the most part Langford's text is quite accessible to the rationalistic Western reader. Her thinking does not seem radically different from this tradition. But there are also eruptions of a different kind of knowledge and a different kind of thinking. This knowledge is not explained or defended by Langford; it is simply stated. It is a tacit resistance to Western ways of thinking.

Other kinds of knowledge which are usually subjugated in the Western literary canon but which come to light in Aboriginal women's life writing are everyday stories about the survival, both in the bush and in high-density urban areas, of people who don't know where the next meal is coming from. Rather than being ashamed of her struggle to survive and the measures she had to take, Langford gives it pride of place in her narrative. We learn, in the course of reading *Don't Take Your Love to Town*, how to make a firebucket — an oven from an empty four-gallon drum, some metal stakes and some bricks in an inner Sydney suburb when you can't pay the gas bill. We learn how women made brooms from ti-trees, how to make damper (Langford, 1988: 269), how to sterilise babies' bottles in the bush, how to live off the bush, and a shopping list of the basics you need to survive in the bush with a large family; how to fish for various kinds of fish even if you can't afford bait, and how to catch and cook porcupine and tortoise. In the context of literature, these knowledges have been considered trivial and inappropriate for inclusion in novels and autobiographies, which are seen as belonging to the domain of high culture. These knowledges emerge discretely and indirectly in the course of the narrative, as resistance to those standards that have dictated what is important and valuable in white middle-class culture, and reveal to the white middle-class reader another way of life – a life as dignified, as tragic or comic, as gripping and as heroic as any we read about in the Western literary canon.

These survival skills are constituted by bush knowledge, both traditional and post-invasion, and homemaking and cooking skills. In the case of the non-traditional knowledge and experience, Aboriginal women shared this with white people who experienced poverty. In fact in *Don't Take Your Love to Town* is a narrative as much about class as it is about gender. Langford makes the point that 'plenty of people lived like that, poor whites as well as blacks' (Langford, 1988: 84). Another Aboriginal woman, Rita Huggins, makes this point about the Brisbane suburb of Inala in her life story, *Auntie Rita* (Huggins and Huggins, 1994: 75).

Aboriginal Language

Another kind of subjugated knowledge is 'lingo' or Aboriginal language. The use of 'lingo' or 'language' affirms a sense of community and shared experience in various contexts, for example when Nobby and James share a cell in jail and Nobby is keen to talk about women and sex (Langford, 1988: 200). This kind of dialogue is very important to Nobby, who we know suffered loneliness and isolation while incarcerated. The words which refer to the police in the text are from Aboriginal languages; the role of the police is a prominent one in many Aboriginal people's lives and they have their own ways of describing and defining the police, words such as 'gungys' (Langford, 1988: 65) and 'gungbul' (Langford, 1988: 262).

Other uses of lingo are for spiritual purposes, such as Ruby's incantation, given to her by her mother, to ward off the spirit of her dead son (Langford, 1988: 160). It is significant that, on this occasion, Ruby becomes deaf after Bill's death and can hear only her mother speak, presumably in lingo. Lingo is also used in tribal stories and songs, for example, the one James Golden sings about the mating of an emu and a kangaroo (Langford, 1988: 139), which Ruby later comically appropriates to describe her own sexuality (Langford, 1988: 126). Other significant uses of lingo refer to traditional foods and animals, cooking and hunting implements (Langford, 1988: 89), and to familial relationships such as those with one's child, sister, brother and grandfather.

In all these examples, use of lingo affirms community and familial bonds and can be seen as a form of resistance to the pressure to speak only English. Aboriginal languages can be used in other resistant ways. There is an interesting example of the pidginisation of the English language where the Aboriginal word 'gubb' (meaning white) is inserted into the English word 'government' to produce 'gubbment' (Langford, 1988: 131).

The sense of family and community is articulated by the narrator of *Don't Take Your Love to Town* in the knowledges of the spirituality of family, in the use of lingo, and in the housekeeping and survival skills: skills that keep a family of ten alive. These knowledges, previously subjugated, rise to the surface in a woman's narrative such as Langford's life story. It is important to read the Aboriginal family in its historical and social context and the role it plays for different generations in resisting white culture. As keepers of the family Aboriginal women are the bearers of subjugated knowledges, a resistance-discourse to white culture. We can thus see that the genre of women's life story is gendered; that is, the life narrative of *Don't Take Your Love to Town* articulates experience and knowledge that can be identified as female. The specificity of this female experience means that the narrative diverges from the largely male tradition of autobiography.

2 Race and Gender: Ruby Langford

Indigenous Life Story and Collectivity

This issue is explored more fully in Susan Stanford Friedman's article 'Women's Autobiographical Selves' (1988). She argues that where men's autobiographies construct a notion of the solitary and privileged individual, women's autobiographies invoke not so much personal and individual histories as collective cultural histories. Langford has said that her book is the story of five generations (stretching from her father's father – Sam Anderson, who was a very significant figure in her life – to her grandchildren) and the changes that have taken place culturally during this time. This notion of the extended family and the role of community and family bonds is an important aspect of Aboriginal women's experience, as it is one way they have maintained coherence and resistance in the face of a dominant culture which continually threatens to erode Aboriginal cultural values and way of life.

The family is not the only unit of the community, as we have seen from the many references to the extended family. There is another sort of community or family that should be mentioned here and that is the spiritual community of elders and apprentices – people with traditional knowledge and law, who keep the knowledge of traditional practices alive. The first person of this kind that the narrative introduces us to is Uncle Ernie Ord, who is an important figure in Ruby's childhood and remains important throughout her life. The narrative closes with Ruby's thoughts about contemporary Aboriginal 'clever people', such as Aunt Millie Boyd, who are the keepers of tribal law and custom. She feels very much part of this community and although she grieves for her loss of tribal language and practices, she affirms the fact that 'there was a direct line from Uncle Ernie Ord to the woman singing the lingo at Yamba, calling the porpoises in, to people like Aunt Millie Boyd' (Langford, 1988: 261), and that she is part of this continuum, this spiritual community which exists across time and space. She celebrates the fact that this spiritual community is alive and well and that there are 'positive forces happening now' (Langford, 1988: 261).

Other theorists who write about the literature of minority groups (see for example Deleuze and Guattari, 1983) have suggested that the autobiographies of women and minority peoples function differently from autobiographies that come from a mainstream, that is, from a white male point of view. The life stories of Indigenous people often foreground the effects of colonisation. In an article in *Writers in Action: The Writers Choice Evenings, Sydney* (1990) Langford relates an anecdote in which her daughter said to her 'Mum, since you wrote your book you're a real political activist', and she replied, 'Pauline, everything pertaining to us Abos has always been political, ever since Cook landed here' (Langford, 1990: 119). The politics of identity is thus an important aspect of contemporary Aboriginal people's lives. The authoring of life stories, the remembering and recording of the past, have an important role in constituting and reconstituting their identity. The process of self-creation and self-consciousness that the narration of life stories represents has a specific political role for Aboriginal people. The politics of identity for marginalised and minority groups is not the same as that of the dominant group, just as the autobiography as a genre functions differently for them: the construction of the self in Indigenous and minority autobiography is seen as a social act which relates to and represents the experience of the community just as much as that of the individual.

It is thus important for us to keep issues such as race, gender and class in mind when we read any Aboriginal text. *Don't Take Your Love to Town*, like many life stories, constructs a notion of the self in the figure of the first-person narrator. This particular narrative is shaped by the contexts of, primarily, race and gender. Because this is the narrative from a minority racialised group we can read in it strategies of resistance to the dominant group, and these strategies are also determined by gender, in this case that of a woman, whose resistance in the face of poverty and racism is played out in the arena of the family.

Difference

What is the relationship between the white reader and an Aboriginal text such as *Don't Take Your Love to Town*? The book articulates a politics of identity along race and gender lines. It articulates the knowledges and experience of a member of a marginalised group that has hitherto been largely invisible and silent in the dominant white culture because of the lack of access Aboriginal people have had to the media and to educational institutions. Literary texts authored by Aboriginal people make them the *subject* of their own experience, identity and knowledge.

Insisting on a constituency's difference means highlighting its 'otherness', which can be neither elided nor appropriated by dominant discourses (here of patriarchy and imperialism). Although otherness is an *effect* of minority groups' economic exploitation, political disenfranchisement and ideological domination, it is also fruitful to talk about it – from the point of view of marginalised groups – as a site of resistance and subversion and thus of empowerment; from this position dominant discourses can be critiqued. An important critical intervention from the margins occurred in white feminism. In the 1970s and 1980s minority and Indigenous women criticised white feminism for failing to take account of the role that race and ethnicity play in in many women's lives. They criticised the way white women assume that their experience is the norm and apply the same value judgements to all women, regardless of the ways in which race or ethnicity shape women's lives and experiences. The erasure or effacement of difference in this process silences and writes out the experience of minority and marginalised women. This is what the black American feminist, Audre Lorde says on the subject of difference:

> Advocating the mere tolerance of difference between women is the grossest reformism. It is a total denial of the creative function of difference in our lives. Difference must be not merely tolerated, but seen as a fund of necessary polarities between which our creativity can spark like a dialectic. (Lorde, 1984: 111)

Furthermore, knowledge itself is made possible, as the critic Gayatri Spivak contends, not by identity, that is, not by 'attempting to "identify" [with] the other as subject in order to know her' (Spivak, 1987: 254) but by a recognition of difference as irreducible and incommensurable. This is not to say of course, that there are not points of commonality with and the possibility of dialogue and exchange between women of different racial and class backgrounds. It is rather to insist that white feminisms recognise that minority and Indigenous women define their own cultural and political agendas and the parameters of these exchanges.

I have argued that the family can be a central site of resistance for Aboriginal people and that it can be a site of power and consolidation for Aboriginal women. I have also suggested that this notion of the family is different from the way many white feminists in the 1970s saw the family in their culture – that is, as a source of the oppression and exploitation of women. In the Introduction I quoted Hazel Carby, a black feminist from the UK, who said that the family had a different role in black communities and thus a different value. Talking about the family is one instance where white feminists may be tempted to read Aboriginal women's life stories according to their own values, rather than listening to what they have to say about their own way of life and respecting the difference of Aboriginal women.

The Politics of Reading

I would like to look at an example of a text which fails to recognise and acknowledge these differences, namely a review of a book by Langford that followed *Don't Take Your Love to Town*, titled *Real Deadly* (1992). The review is by Mary Rose Liverani and was published in *The Australian* in March 1992. In this review Liverani makes a series of moral judgements about the narrator's lifestyle. She foregrounds the fact that Langford was not married to the fathers of her children, who were products of 'de facto unions' (unfortunately she gets her facts wrong here, as Langford did marry one of these men, namely Peter Langford), and goes on to comment that Langford's family seem to live on fast food rather than 'home cooking', implying that Langford's homemaking skills and parental responsibilities seem to be lacking. She abhors the party behaviour of the family and suggests that the 'mistress of the house's' proper concern should be in 'creating an attractive home' rather than having riotous fun and encouraging 'pack behaviour'. We can see here a prejudice against Aboriginal people assembling in large numbers, a tendency noted earlier when I discussed the way that the Housing Commission tried to break up Aboriginal communities and to integrate them into the white community by giving them houses in white suburbs. Liverani is judging this book and the 'way of life' of the Langford family through the lens of white middle-class people.

Black writer Mudrooroo (Colin Johnson) has written a review of Liverani's review. He points to the fact that Aboriginal literature, which often has working-class origins, is mediated by the middle class. In other words, not only publishers, but also many reviewers, read Aboriginal literature through the lens of their own expectations and their own values, which are often middle class; they often have 'an abysmal ignorance of Aboriginal culture' (Mudrooroo, 1992–3: 379). He makes the comment that Liverani and Langford are 'separated by a great gulf: of race, of class' (Mudrooroo, 1992–3: 382) and follows this up with the important point that 'the reading of Aboriginal Literature [must] be learnt' (Mudrooroo, 1992–3: 378). It is with this point in mind that I have been focusing in this chapter on how we read Aboriginal texts and suggesting strategies we can deploy when reading texts from minority and marginalised groups.

When non-Indigenous readers are blind to their own values which are determined by race, class, age, sexual preference, regional identity and so on, they may simply be judging texts by these standards. When they recognise difference, however, they may learn something new not only about Aboriginal people but also about Australia's colonial history. Much of this history has been repressed because it was so violent. Benedict Anderson has said that most people experience a kind of 'cultural amnesia' about the past. He says that when a country's history cannot be remembered it must be narrated (Anderson, 1991). And the people who can narrate this history of violence for non-Indigenous Australians (and others) are precisely those who have been oppressed – Aboriginal people.

Clearly, many 'settler' Australians in particular (those who are now several generations removed from frontier violence) want to understand the legacies of the past and the way they impact upon contemporary Aboriginal people. As mentioned before, sales of Sally Morgan's *My Place* have reached over 500,000. *Don't Take Your Love to Town* has sold at least 20,000 copies, also a high figure. These figures indicate how popular Aboriginal texts have become, and the fact that non-Aboriginal Australians (and indeed global audiences) recognise the importance of learning about the past and the present from Aboriginal points of view.

The Educative Role of Aboriginal Women

One question that we should ask ourselves in relation to books from minority and marginalised groups such as Aboriginal writers is: what audience do these writers have in mind? Several Aboriginal writers have made the comment that they write for both a white and an Aboriginal audience. Alice Nannup, who lived in Geraldton, Western Australia, has said that one of the main reasons she published her autobiography, *When the Pelican Laughed* (1992), was to record her life history and the history of the Moore River Mission, and that she wanted this story to be passed on to her grandchildren.

As well as writing for their own family, Aboriginal women also speak to non-Indigenous Australians. They see their role as that of educating both their own family and non-Indigenous Australians generally. Aboriginal women's life stories are an 'education' for the contemporary generation of Aboriginal people, those who have not lived through the times related by the grandmothers and who, in some cases, did not even know they had Aboriginal heritage until late in their childhood (even though their family history bore ample evidence of the transgenerational impact of the racialised management of Aboriginal people), as was the case with Sally Morgan and Patsy Cohen (Cohen and Somerville, 1990: 34). Ruby Langford makes the point that Aboriginal writing and oral storytelling has an important role in the Aboriginal community when she talks about her third book, which focuses on the Bundjalung people of New South Wales. She says:

> In doing [research on] the Bundjalung people we are gaining expertise, and we are educating the Aboriginal people as well ... Aboriginal people get so little recognition in this country that it's vital that both Kooris and Gubbas [white people] learn about our plight and our condition. (Langford, 1991: 130)

Much Aboriginal literature is therefore aimed as much at a white audience (and perhaps non-Indigenous audiences more broadly) as an Aboriginal one, as several Aboriginal writers have commented. This is partly a marketing strategy – there are not enough Aboriginal readers to support Aboriginal writers – but more importantly, as I have mentioned, there is a driving urge on the part of many writers to break the silence, the 'cultural amnesia' of white Australia, to borrow Anderson's phrase. Langford has been outspoken on this issue, and talks about white Australians' ignorance quite angrily:

> The Australian people don't know a damn thing about . . . what Governments of the past have done to the Aboriginal people of this country; and some don't even want to know of the shameful history of our past and our present. (Langford, 1990: 118)

She elaborates further about the period up until the 1990s:

> Some people do not understand what the word, mission, means. I'm totally devastated that nothing has been taught in the school curriculum about Aboriginal culture and history. (Langford, 1992b: 8)

She sees books like *Don't Take Your Love to Town* as redressing this process in some small way:

> My story is about twentieth century Aboriginal life . . . About the way we live today. And it's probably the only information that a lot of students get that puts the Aboriginal point of view. Because Koori history and culture is almost never taught in schools, and if it is, it is usually as it is seen by whites, and not from an Aboriginal perspective. (Langford, 1991: 129)

She reiterates the point that Aboriginal women's life stories are important because they articulate an Aboriginal version of history. They construct an Aboriginal identity from an Aboriginal point of view, asserting themselves as *subjects* of their own experience, knowledge and literature rather than being the *object* of white people's definitions.

Conclusion

What I have aimed to do in this chapter is to examine how Aboriginal women's life stories, taking *Don't Take Your Love to Town* as a representative example, articulate particularised forms of Aboriginality. I have suggested that a reading practice that takes account of difference is important, taking Liverani's review as an example of one way of reading Aboriginal literature that does not. It is important, for example, that we are aware of the stereotypes of Aboriginal people in the media, such as in newspaper reviews. Ruby Langford has said:

> We are sick of being forever stereotyped as lazy, layabout drunks and no-hopers. You just have to look at the television to see how the negative image of the Aboriginal people is maintained. (Langford, 1991: 130)

Recent publications by Aboriginal authors present different images and a different understanding of contemporary Aboriginal people. They portray what Langford has called the 'positive forces that are happening now' (Langford, 1991: 261). She describes the writing of *Don't Take Your Love to Town* not only as a journey of self-discovery but also a reaching out to white people in particular, and it is appropriate that she has the last word here:

> when I finished this book a weight would be lifted from my mind, not only because I could examine my own life from it and know who I was, but because it may help better the relationship between the Aboriginal and white people. (Langford, 1991: 269)

3
Family and Storytelling in Alice Nannup's *When The Pelican Laughed*

The Family

In Aboriginal women's life stories we can observe gender-specific strategies of resistance to white racism such as the maintenance of the family and a distinct way of life. This has been in response to past governments' policy (the 'Aborigines Protection Acts') of removing fair-skinned children from Aboriginal families, placing them in missions and reserves and later sending them to work with white city-dwellers as domestics or with white farmers as domestics and station workers where they were often used virtually as slave labour. Roberta Sykes has described the forced removal of these children from their families as 'a major crime against Aboriginal people and humanity generally, and ... arguably the most despicable white activity of the past century' (Sykes, 1991: 181).

In *When the Pelican Laughed* (1992), we can see the effects of the *Aborigines Act 1905* (WA) on Alice Nannup's life. She describes being taken away from her family in the Pilbara region of northern Western Australia and working as an unpaid or underpaid domestic from the age of twelve (at Moore River Native Settlement and in private homes, including that of A. O. Neville, the WA Chief Protector of Aborigines). Of this Act she says: 'they wanted to disconnect people from their past'

(Nannup, 1992: 70) and 'they meant for us to never find our way back home' (120). Nannup's story culminates in her finally finding her 'way back home' at the age of fifty-four; 'they might have taken me away from my home, but they didn't take my home away from me' she says (204).

During the period of assimilation from the late 1930s through to the mid-1960s, the government wanted to resocialise Aboriginal people as white Australians. Aboriginal families were one place where Aboriginal values and culture survived the social coercion to assimilate. For Nannup, the home and her family – specifically her mother – were a source of comfort. Nannup, for example, talks with pride about her mother's cooking and her own (traditional and white). She describes how, even when living in poverty and with few facilities on the Aboriginal reserve in Geraldton (a coastal town in Western Australia), she was able to make a special meal for her family on Sundays:

> Living on the reserve had its disadvantages, but we always tried to make the best of a bad situation. Every Sunday we'd have a hot dinner – even if it was just a hard-up stew. That was a stew I used to make where you just threw everything in – onions, potatoes, rice or barley – and left it to steam. It had no meat so I used to make dumplings to pop in, and flavour it up with a bit of Worcestershire sauce. It used to turn out really nice, too. I'd also make up spotted dog for after. Spotted dog is made from flour, with a bit of dripping, sultanas, some lemon peeling and golden syrup. You mix all that together, then wrap it up in a calico cloth and boil it up for a few hours. I had to put it on at six o'clock in the morning for it to be ready by twelve. (Nannup, 1992: 183)

The language used to describe the food here is specific and colourful in all its detail. We can also see the marks of oral storytelling in this passage in phrases like 'you just threw everything in', 'it used to turn out really nice, too', 'I used to make spotted dog for after' and 'you mix all that together'. This vernacular style creates the intimate atmosphere of a personal conversation between the reader and the narrator and draws us into Nannup's narrative of everyday life.

3 Family and Storytelling: Alice Nannup

By contrast, the food that Aboriginal people were forced to eat at the Moore River Native Settlement, where meals were provided by the Settlement kitchens, was 'disgusting'. For example:

> For the soup they'd cook up these awful sheep heads. First they'd skin them, but never take the eyes out, then they'd split them down the middle, give them a quick rinse and throw them in the copper. Sometimes those sheep heads had bott-fly in their noses but they wouldn't worry about that. They'd just throw it in and we'd see that in our soup. (Nannup, 1992: 64)

This disgusting food, Nannup says, was a tactic 'to deliberately lower us; well, degrade us really'. She asserts with pride: 'I wasn't brought up like that. My mother was a beautiful cook and we ate lovely meals back home' (Nannup, 1992: 64).

As well as tasks such as cooking, Nannup talks about other domestic practices such as the effectiveness of traditional health cures such as goanna fat and emu oil (Nannup, 1992: 217) and the power of spirituality. Nannup's mother is her link with Aboriginal spirituality: she assigns the young Alice her totem, the jutarrara or pelican (Nannup, 1992: 30). Through the narrative Nannup affirms the power of the spiritual world and its intervention in her life at times of crisis, such as the pebbles that warn her of the death of her sister and mother (Nannup, 1992: 156), and the bird call that warns her of her daughter Margaret's death (Nannup, 1992: 168). She describes the former event thus:

> One night I was sitting up feeding Ron, when a pebble came in under the tent door. Will saw me staring at it and he said, 'What are you looking at?'
> 'I don't know for sure, it's a sign.' (Nannup, 1992: 156)

This pebble is followed by two others. Nannup says, 'I didn't know what it meant, or who it was from, but I knew it was meant for me' (Nannup, 1992: 157). A few days later she met an old friend who told her that her sister and mother had died. 'All the way home my heart was heavy with grief, and all I could think about was the three pebbles that had been sent to warn me,' she says (Nannup, 1992: 158). She concludes the narrative of *When the Pelican Laughed* with an affirmation of Aboriginal law when she visits a pool in her family country and appeases the old snake spirit (Nannup, 1992: 223): 'That's beautiful isn't it?' she says, 'To keep your tradition and never let it go' (Nannup, 1992: 224).

Another example of her links with the traditional way of life and her resistance to white socialisation is her use of Aboriginal language. She relates how first her white father (Nannup, 1992: 27) and then officials at the Moore River Mission (Nannup, 1992: 85) forbade her use of 'language'. In opposition to these directives the children found in their native tongue a form of resistance and a means to curse the people who took them from their parents:

> we used to curse those Campbells. We used to say to each other in language that they were terrible for taking us away from our home, and we wished something would happen to them. Oh, we used to be nasty. (Nannup, 1992: 56)

One effect of separating children from each other was to diminish the use of Aboriginal language, and Nannup describes how she lost her knowledge of the language in this way (Nannup, 1992: 92). She also describes how, despite broken promises to send her to school, she learnt to write English by copying jam labels. She is very proud of this subversive tactic and relates this story several times (Nannup, 1992: 122, 189). Being able to write enables her to keep in touch with friends, a privilege that had been denied her as a child when her white 'employers' refused to reply to her family's letters (she herself was then unable to read or write).

In their constitution of family life Aboriginal women's life stories are laced with descriptions of the practice of home making, and talk about traditional foods and cooking, health remedies and wisdom, as we have seen from Nannup's narrative. The naming of recipes, of bush tucker and health remedies, like the naming Aboriginal language groups or nations, is an important act of decolonisation, of reinscribing domestic and geographical space from an Aboriginal woman's point of view. The construction of a genealogy of the family is also a process of naming, of articulating what Michel Foucault called 'subjugated knowledges' which are 'located low down on the hierarchy, beneath the required level of cognition or scientificity' (Foucault, 1980: 82).

As well as the naming of domestic practices, we see in these life stories that the storytellers' naming of themselves is an important act of decolonisation and of reclaiming the past and their heritage. Nannup tells us her Aboriginal name, Wari (Nannup, 1992: 20), her skin group, garimarra (Nannup, 1992: 35), and the name of her mother's people (Yindjibarndi) and the languages she spoke (Nannup, 1992: 20). In *My Bundjalung People* Ruby Langford tells us how her aunty gave her the name Ginibi, which means black swan, and which she had used since 1992, combined with her European name. This name affirms her link with the Bundjalung people. Other Aboriginal women life-story authors such as Elsie Roughsey (Labumore) and Doris Pilkington (Garimara) use their Aboriginal name alongside their European one to point to their dual heritage.

Strategies of resistance were of paramount importance given the intensive surveillance of Aboriginal people. On the missions Aboriginal people were subjected to restriction of movement, a prohibition on mixing with family (the older people) and the regimentation of their time. When they became working people outside the mission, the Department of Aboriginal Affairs exercised control of their money (Nannup, 1992: 118), their movements, and who they could work for; and it could intervene in their personal lives and interrogate them at any time (Nannup, 1992: 188). And yet, Nannup relates bitterly, the Department did not even inform her of the death of family members (Nannup, 1992: 179). Throughout her narrative Nannup deplores the lack of rights of Aboriginal people; she repeatedly refers to herself and other Aboriginal people as 'slaves'. Of her childhood spent living with white people on a farm near Beeginup as their servant and doing household and farm chores she says, 'looking back, they didn't have us there as kids, they had us as slaves' (Nannup, 1992: 52). She uses the word 'slaves' because, although they were paid a very small wage, this was often taken from them for misdemeanours such as taking more than ten minutes to do the dishes. Nannup's life between the ages of fourteen and twenty-one, which she spent on the Moore River Native Settlement, was no better. 'Really, all I ever did there was work,' she says (Nannup, 1992: 69).

> All the girls who were taken out of school and sent down to the sewing room, were started off on button holing and things like that. We had no choice about working there and we were never paid for it. We'd work a full week, then we'd go down every Saturday morning to clean the machines, brush them and oil them up ready for Monday. Then they'd come along with a little block of chocolate for us and that was our pay. (Nannup, 1992: 70)

Later in her life Nannup and several other young women run away from Ida Valley Station near Leonora because of the hard work. When the manager finally tracks them down and tries to take them back Nannup says to him: 'We were just slaves there and we want to go' (Nannup, 1992: 143). She describes how hard life was at this station and the farm she lived on as a child:

> Thinking back, I'd say Beeginup and Ida Valley were the two places where I was the most flat out. It was really terrible. All of us – Jess, Mary and myself – were just worked and worked. I was supposed to get five shillings a week there but they never paid me. They never paid any of us ... It was all too much. (Nannup, 1992: 141)

Storytelling

Late in her life, at the age of seventy-eight, Alice Nannup was able to produce her own narrative of the historical events, such as the Aborigines Protection Acts, which shaped her life. That this action is politically important to her she asserts several times. She sees the book as an important documentation of the past both for her family's sake and for the rewriting of history. Of the latter she wryly remarks: 'You won't find anything about the hell we went through in history books, but it happened, every little bit of it is true' (Nannup, 1992: 218). Her stories, she explains, are already circulating within her family, and part of her motivation in getting the book together is to consolidate their history: 'I think it's been important to get all my stories down into the one book. That way my family, and their family, and their family, and so on, will always have them' (Nannup, 1992: 217). But she also wants to make

3 Family and Storytelling: Alice Nannup

her story public knowledge and to acquaint others with the history of Aboriginal people under colonisation: '[I] hope that all people, young, old, black, white, will read this book and see how life was for people in my time' (Nannup, 1992: 218).

Walter Benjamin suggests that storytelling is an essentially social act which rests upon 'the ability to exchange experiences' (Benjamin, 1973: 83) and to offer counsel to the listener. Companionship, he suggests, is an important aspect of storytelling. The sense of exchanging not simply information but experience, and that of giving counsel, are evident in Nannup's narrative, for example in the 'moral' of her many tales of self-assertion (Nannup, 1992: 14–6, 117–8, 191–2) and in the advice she gives to her children and, by extension, to other Aboriginal people experiencing racism, such as: 'I taught my kids to stand up for themselves, and not let other people treat them like dirt on account of being Aboriginal' (Nannup, 1992: 191).

Benjamin suggests that storytelling is drawn from 'the realm of living speech' (Benjamin, 1973: 87), a feature also apparent in Nannup's narrative. He says that storytelling is the 'art of repeating stories' (91) and is made up of 'layers of a variety of retellings' (93); Nannup sees her stories as narratives that will be repeatedly retold and reread in her family. Her own narrative, for example, opens with the narrator repeating stories her mother had told her (Nannup, 1992: 18).

The giving of counsel is evident in the enunciative mode of the Aboriginal narratives (that is, the context and manner in which they are originally narrated). These narratives are often didactic (drawing a moral from a particular story or incident) and occasionally address the listener/reader directly. The narratives frequently use the vocative voice (that is, addressing the reader as 'you') and are cast in a mode that invokes the active presence of the listener/reader. They are performative acts shaped to meet the social requirements and conditions of the occasion. We can see how narratives such as *When the Pelican Laughed* are drawn from 'the realm of living speech' and how they function to exchange experience and give counsel in the following passage:

> I grilled my kids from when they were knee-high to a grasshopper. I told them I didn't want them to grow up and have to fight their way through life like I had to. I wanted them to do better for themselves.

> 'Whenever opportunity knocks,' I said, 'don't knock it back, grasp it with both hands, because it's your future, and you're not going to have me all your life to defend and take care of you,' and they have done just that. (Nannup, 1992: 218)

Throughout the narrative we are aware of the colloquial language that is definitive of the oral nature of many Aboriginal women's life stories. Phrases like 'knee-high to a grasshopper' are suggestive of everyday conversation and remind us that the narrative of *When the Pelican Laughed* is transcribed from taped interviews. The oral language of this passage conveys the intimacy, the humour and the liveliness of an entertaining storyteller; we feel we are sitting down with Alice Nannup as she relates the stories of her family. There is also a simplicity and directness in her language; in this passage she tells of the difficulty and the struggle of her life without being overwhelmed by self-pity or pathos. We can also see the pedagogic impulse of her storytelling in this passage and the way in which she intends the various stories of her life to act as examples for younger Aboriginal people, especially in dealing with racialised aggression. In one anecdote she relates how while living in Perth, young Aboriginal women were often called derogatory sexualised and racialised names such as 'dark clouds' and 'black velvet'. She describes in a story that is both amusing and proud about how they retaliated on one occasion, trading insults and giving the white men harassing them 'our tuppence worth'. One of the young women says, 'they're not going to call me names, not going to insult me' (Nannup, 1992: 118).

Many Aboriginal women see their role in recording their life histories as educative. They see themselves as educators of both black and white people, and as archivists and custodians of their family history. They produce their narratives with the conscious intent of recording and conveying Aboriginal knowledge. In order to do this these women collaborate with editors, publishers and interviewers. In Nannup's case, she worked with two younger people, one of whom was related to her. They interviewed her and transcribed the interviews (which consisted of family stories), which were then edited by the publisher's editor. In this way we can see that Aboriginal women's life stories such as *When the Pelican Laughed* are a combination of oral and written record. We can see evidence of the oral nature of her narrative; the narrative has been transformed into written form without erasing the marks of its oral genesis.

Recollection and the Past

The telling and retelling of stories has a political importance for minority and marginalised groups. It organises consciousness and creates a social and collective memory. We are aware from narratives like Sally Morgan's *My Place* that some Aboriginal people have grown up not knowing they are Aboriginal (Patsy Cohen relates a similar story in her book *Ingelba and the Five Black Matriarchs* [1990]). Many others have grown up not knowing the history of their people or the life stories of their parents and grandparents. Aboriginal women who produce life stories do so with the aim of creating a history and a record of the past, hence the inclusion of details about domestic practices and family members. The very act of collecting, organising and writing down these stories transforms the past into history and heritage. It is this heritage that contemporary Aboriginal people find crucial to affirm, and women's life stories are an important part of this process of reclaiming the past. On the back cover of Alice Nannup's book, for example, Sally Morgan writes that 'through her book [Nannup] has passed on a precious heritage'. The documenting of subjugated knowledges from everyday life, for example, is a principle method in life stories of bringing the past alive.

Aboriginal women's life stories record and celebrate the survival of the family and the subjugated knowledges of traditional and contemporary domestic, healing and spiritual practices. In addition to the survival of the family these narratives record a past which narrates a history of hard work, disempowerment, dispossession and the severance of links with earlier generations. I have mentioned in the chapter on Sally Morgan how Daisy Corunna tells her granddaughter that she has been 'a work animal' all her life. Alice Nannup also tells of her many years of domestic and farm labour from the age of twelve onwards; 'we had to scrub, polish, cook or work out in the fields like a man', she says (Nannup, 1992: 218). She describes her book, *When the Pelican Laughed*, as a record of 'just how hard I had to work in my day' (Nannup, 1992: 217). These women's lives of hard work are combined with a lack of power and control over their lives. As single women, for example, they were monitored and supervised by the Departments of Aborigines; they had 'no say' and 'no choice' about the work they had to do when they left the missions (Nannup, 1992: 218). (This recalls the title of Rosemary van den Berg's life story, *No Options! No Choice!* which is about her father who was taken to Moore River Native Settlement.) Alice Nannup's life story, like those of other Aboriginal women, is one of recollection, a (re)reading of the narrator's own life, often punctuated with a sense of amazement and disbelief at the injustices she and other Aboriginal people endured. Phrases such as 'looking back' (Nannup, 1992: 52), 'when I think back' (Nannup, 1992: 71) and 'thinking back' (Nannup, 1992: 141) establish Nannup's speaking position as retrospective. She is re-evaluating the past from the perspective of the present and its clearly changed conditions for Aboriginal people. Her powerlessness as a child, an adolescent and a struggling mother, contrasts with her present status as the progenitor of one hundred children, grandchildren and great-grandchildren (Nannup, 1992: 218), a prodigal daughter reunited with her family in the Pilbara after years of absence, and a published author. She speaks with the authority of a matriarch and a person who has re-established her links with family and country. This contrasts markedly with the lack of dignity and respect accorded to her as a younger woman. She describes how the Department of Aborigines and white employers, for example, infantilised Aboriginal women in their twenties and thirties by referring to them as 'girls' (Nannup, 1992: 101, 117).

Many of the older Aboriginal women life-story writers and tellers write from a position of power and status both in white Australian and Aboriginal communities. Many of the women I mentioned in the Introduction who were born in the 1930s, for example, became political leaders during the 1960s, especially those on the east coast. Mabel Edmund and Ellie Gaffney, in particular, had high-profile political careers, Edmund being a Shire Councillor, a Federal Commissioner and an endorsed Labor Party candidate. In 1986 she was made a Member of the Order of Australia. Gaffney also had a high profile in Aboriginal affairs, mainly in the nursing and education fields and in Aboriginal media organisations in Queensland. Shirley Smith and Margaret Tucker, two other Aboriginal women who have published autobiographies, were awarded Member of the Most Excellent Order of the British Empire (MBEs). Many of these women have a high community profile and some, like Langford Ginibi, appeared regularly in the media. Several went through tertiary education after they had raised their families (for example, Alice Nannup, Patsy Cohen, Doris Pilkington and Evelyn Crawford). It is clear then that they were writing and speaking from a position of prestige, authority and achievement, and that their work is the pedagogic articulation of an oppressed history.

Their awards and recognition, that is, their personal success, highlights the huge gulf between the present and the past. This leads to a sense of anger over the injustices of the past. The memory of their lives as younger women produces a sense of anger at their disempowerment. The connection with the past is very important as it affirms a connection with the past generations of family and also a sense of belonging and of home. But as I suggested in the Introduction, reliving and remembering the past also means living with a sense of loss. This sense of loss is most acute in *When the Pelican Laughed* when Nannup first returns to the Pilbara after many years absence and, in the middle of the night, passes by the station where her mother, sister and little nephew were buried; 'it was so sad to pass them all by in the night, and it really rang home that I was never, ever, going to see any of them again' (Nannup, 1992: 207–8). While she was living down south Nannup was distanced emotionally from the loss of her family; the act of returning was an act of acknowledging the fact of their death. This sadness is mixed with anger, and to remember the past is also to acknowledge the severance from her culture and her family:

> Somedays, when I think about things, there is a lot of grief and sadness in my heart. It's then that I realise how much I was denied when I was taken away. (Nannup, 1992: 211)

Nannup says she felt 'cheated' and 'deprived of so much' (Nannup, 1992: 209). We can see here that memory is political; in reliving and remembering the past Aboriginal people bond together through the common experience of injustice. The mixture of sadness and anger that we see in this passage fuels much of Aboriginal people's efforts to retell the black history of Australia which has been all but erased from non-Aboriginal Australians' memory and history.

Works Cited

Amos, Valerie and Pratibha Parmar (1984). 'Challenging Imperial Feminism', *Feminist Review* 17, Autumn, pp. 3–19.
Anderson, Benedict (1991). *Imagined Communities,* London: Verso.
Attwood, Bain (1992). 'Portrait of an Aboriginal as an Artist: Sally Morgan and the Construction of Aboriginality', *Australian Historical Studies* 25, 99, pp. 302–18.
Bayet-Charlton, Fabienne (2002). *Finding Ullagundahi Island,* Crows Nest, NSW: Allen & Unwin.
Behrendt, Larissa (2004). *Home,* St Lucia, Qld.: University of Queensland Press.
Behrendt, Larissa (2009). *Legacy,* St Lucia, Qld.: University of Queensland Press.
Benjamin, Walter (1973). *Illuminations,* New York: Schocken.
Brewster, Anne (2015). *Giving this Country a Memory: Contemporary Aboriginal Voices of Australia,* New York: Cambria Press.
Burke, Peter (1989). 'History as Social Memory', in Thomas Butler (ed.), *Memory: History, Culture and the Mind,* Oxford: Basil Blackwell, pp. 97–113.
Burney, Linda (1994). 'An Aboriginal Way of Being Australian', *Australian Feminist Studies* 19, pp. 17–24.
Carby, Hazel V. (1982). 'White woman listen! Black feminism and the boundaries of sisterhood', in Race and Politics Group, Centre for Cultural Studies (ed.), *The Empire Strikes Back: Race and Racism in 70s Britain,* Birmingham: University of Birmingham Centre for Contemporary Cultural Studies, pp. 212–35.
Clare, Monica (1978). *Karobran,* Sydney: Alternative Publishing Cooperative.

Cohen, Patsy and Margaret Somerville (1990). *Ingelba and the Five Black Matriarchs,* Sydney: Allen & Unwin.
Coleman, Dylan (2012). *Mazin' Grace,* St Lucia, Qld.: University of Queensland Press.
Cowlishaw, Gillian (1987). 'Colour, Culture and the Aboriginalists', *Man* 22, pp. 221-37.
Crawford, Evelyn (1993). *Over My Tracks,* Ringwood: Penguin.
Daylight, Phyllis and Mary Johnstone (1986). *Women's Business: Report of the Women's Task Force,* Canberra: Australian Government Publishing Service.
Deleuze, Gilles and Felix Guattari (1983). 'What is a Minor Literature?', *Mississippi Review* 22, 3, pp. 13-33.
Donaldson, Tamsin (1991). 'Australian Tales of Mystery and Miscegenation', *Meanjin* 50, pp. 341-52.
Dudgeon, Patricia and Darlene Oxenham (1989). 'The Complexity of Aboriginal Diversity: Identity and Kindredness', *Black Voices* 5, 1, pp. 22-39.
Dudgeon, Patricia, Glenys Grogan and Darlene Oxenham (1995). 'Learning Identities and Differences', in Luke Carmen (ed.), *Feminisms and Pedagogies of Everyday Life,* Albany: State University of New York Press, pp. 1-30.
Edmund, Mabel (1992). *No Regrets,* St Lucia, Qld.: University of Queensland Press.
Ferrier, Carole (1992). 'Aboriginal Women's Narratives' in Carole Ferrier (ed.), *Gender, Politics and Fiction,* 2nd edn, St Lucia, Qld.: University of Queensland Press, pp. 200-218.
Fesl, Eve (1993). 'Eve Fesl' , in Stuart Rintoul (ed.), *The Wailing: A National Black Oral History,* Melbourne: Heinemann, pp. 339-41.
Fielder, John (1991). 'Postcoloniality and Mudrooroo Narogin's Ideology of Aboriginality' *SPAN* 32, April, pp. 43-50.
Fisher, Bev (1977). 'Race and Class: Beyond Personal Politics' *Quest* 3, 4, Spring, pp. 2-14.
Foucault, Michel (1980). *Power/Knowledge: Selected Interviews and Other Writings 1972-1977,* Colin Gordon (ed.), trans. Colin Gordon, Leo Marshall, John Mepham, Kate Soper. New York: Pantheon.
Friedman, Susan Stanford (1988). 'Women's Autobiographical Selves: Theory and Practice', in Shari Benstock (ed.), *The Private Self Theory and Practice of Women's Autobiographical Writings,* London: Routledge, pp. 10-33.
Gaffney, Ellie (1989). *Somebody Now,* Canberra: Aboriginal Studies Press.
Gelder, Ken (1991). 'Aboriginal Narrative and Property', *Meanjin* 50, 2-3, pp. 353-65.
Graham, Duncan (1989). 'A Question of Place', *Sydney Morning Herald Good Weekend,* September 16, pp. 54-8.

Works Cited

Haag, Oliver (2011). 'Indigenous Australian Autobiography and the Question of Genre: an Analysis of Scholarly Discourse', *Acta Neophilologica* 44, 1–2, pp. 69–80.

Heiss, Anita (2001). *Who am I?: the Diary of Mary Talence*, Lindfield, NSW: Scholastic Press.

Hooton, Joy (1990). *Stories of Herself When Young: Autobiographies of Childhood by Australian Women*, Melbourne: Oxford University Press.

Horáková, Martina (2011). 'Indigenous Collaborative Life Writing: Narrative Transgression in *Auntie Rita* and *Kayang & Me*', in Stephen Paul Hardy, Martina Horáková, Michael Matthew Kaylor, Kateřina Prajznerová (eds.), *Alternatives in Biography: Writing Lives in Diverse English-Language Contexts*, Brno: Masaryk University Press, pp. 91–138.

Horton, Wesley (1988). 'Australian Aboriginal Writers: Partially Annotated Bibliography of Australian Aboriginal Writers 1924–1987', in Anna Rutherford (ed.), *Aboriginal Culture Today*, Sydney: Dangaroo.

Huggins, Jackie (1991). 'Towards A Biography of Rita Huggins', in Ivor Indyk and Elizabeth Webby (eds.), *Memory, Southerly Special Issue* 3, pp. 143–64.

Huggins, Jackie (1993). 'Always Was Always Will Be', *Australian Historical Studies* 25, 100, pp. 459–64.

Huggins, Jackie and Rita Huggins (1994). *Auntie Rita*, Canberra: Aboriginal Studies Press.

Illing, Dorothy (1994). 'Taking Back Your History', *Campus Review*, August, 4–10, pp. 1–2.

Janke, Terri (2005). *Butterfly Song*, Camberwell, Vic.: Penguin Books.

Johnson, Eva (1991). 'What Do They Call Me?', in Dale Spender (ed.), *Heroines*, Ringwood: Penguin, pp. 237–55.

Jones, Jennifer (2009). *Black Writers, White Editors*, Melbourne: Australian Scholarly Publishing.

Kennedy, Marnie (1985). *Born a Half-Caste*, Canberra: Australian Institute of Aboriginal Studies.

Kennedy, Rosanne (2008). 'Subversive Witnessing: Mediating Indigenous Testimony in Australian Cultural and Legal Institutions', *Women's Studies Quarterly* 36, 1 & 2, pp 58–75.

Langford, Ruby (1988). *Don't Take Your Love to Town*, Ringwood: Penguin.

Langford, Ruby (Ginibi) (1990). 'Don't Take Your Love to Town', in Gerry Turcotte (ed.) *Writers in Action: The Writers Choice Evenings*, Sydney: Currency Press, pp. 113–37.

Langford, Ruby (Ginibi) (1991). 'Koori Dubays', in Dale Spender (ed.) *Heroines*, Ringwood: Penguin, pp. 129–41.

Langford, Ruby (1992a). *Real Deadly*, Sydney: Angus & Robertson.

Langford, Ruby (1992b). 'Tracing my Roots' *The Independent Monthly* December–January, pp. 8.
Langford, Ruby (1994a). *My Bundjalung People*, St Lucia, Qld.: University of Queensland Press.
Langford, Ruby (1994b). 'It's Our Turn: An Interview with Ruby Langford Ginibi', interview with Caitlin McGrath and Philippa Sawyer, *Meridian* 13, 1, pp. 79–87.
Langford, Ruby (1994c). 'Talking with Ruby Langford Ginibi', interview with Janine Little, *Hecate* 20, l, pp. 101–21.
Langford, Ruby (1994d). 'Nobby's Story', *Meanjin* 53, pp. 51–60.
Langton, Marcia (1994). 'Aboriginal art and film: the politics of representation', *Race and Class* 35, 4, April–June, pp. 89–106.
Lattas, Andrew (1993). 'Essentialism, Memory and Resistance', *Oceania* 63, 3, pp. 240–67.
Leane, Jeanine (2012). 'Threads and Secrets: Australian Aboriginal Women's Life History Writing 1988-2012.' *The Southern Hemisphere Review* 28, 1, pp. 4–17.
Liverani, Mary Rose (1992). 'From Outside, Without Insight', *Weekend Australian* 28-9 March, pp. 6.
Lorde, Audre (1984). 'The Master's Tools Will Never Dismantle the Master's House', *Sister Outsider*, New York: The Crossing Press, pp. 110–13.
MacDermott, Doireann (1984). *Autobiographical & Biographical Writing in the Commonwealth*, Barcelona: Editorial AUSA.
Merlan, Francesca (1988). 'Gender in Aboriginal Social Life: A Review', in R. M. Berndt and R. Tonkinson (eds.), *Social Anthropology and Australian Aboriginal Studies,* Canberra: Aboriginal Studies Press, pp. 15–76.
Michaels, Eric (1988). 'Para-ethnography' *Art and Text* 30, September–November, pp. 42–51.
Morgan, Sally (1987). *My Place,* Fremantle: Fremantle Arts Centre Press.
Morgan, Sally (1988). 'A Fundamental Question of Identity, an Interview with Sally Morgan', Interview with Mary Wright, Anna Rutherford (ed.), *Aboriginal Culture Today,* Sydney: Dangaroo, pp. 93–109.
Morgan, Sally (1989). *Wanamurraganya: The Story of Jack McPhee,* Fremantle: Fremantle Arts Centre Press.
Morgan, Sally (1992). 'Interview with Sally Morgan', in Interview with Delys Bird and Dennis Haskell, Delys Bird and Dennis Haskell (eds.), *Whose Place? A Study of Sally Morgan's My Place,* Sydney: Angus & Robertson, pp. 1–22.
Morris, Barry (1989). *Domesticating Resistance: The Dhan-Gadi Aborigines and the Australian State*, Oxford: Berg Publishers.
Mudrooroo (Narogin) (1990). *Writing from the Fringe: A Study of Modern Aboriginal Literature*, Melbourne: Hyland House Publishing.

Works Cited

Mudrooroo (1992). 'A Literature of Aboriginality', *Ulitarra* 1, pp. 28–33.

Mudrooroo (Nyoongah) (1992–3). 'Couldn't Ya Cry, If Ya Couldn't Laugh: The Literature of Aboriginality and its Reviewers', *SPAN* 34–35, pp. 376–83.

Muecke, Stephen (1992). *Textual Spaces: Aboriginality and Cultural Studies*, Sydney: New South Wales University Press.

Munkara, Marie (2009). *Every Secret Thing*, St Lucia, Qld.: University of Queensland Press.

Nannup, Alice (with Lauren Marsh and Stephen Kinnane) (1992). *When the Pelican Laughed*, Fremantle: Fremantle Arts Centre Press.

Pearson, Noel (1994). 'A Troubling Inheritance', *Race and Class* 35, 4, April–June, pp. 1–9.

Nunukul, Oodgeroo (1972). *Stradbroke Dreamtime*, Pymble: Angus & Robertson.

Pilkington, Doris (1991). *Caprice: A Stockman's Daughter*, St Lucia, Qld: University of Queensland Press.

Pilkington, Doris (1996). *Follow the Rabbit-Proof Fence*, St Lucia, Qld.: University of Queensland Press.

Read, Peter (1989). 'Introduction', in Coral Edwards and Peter Read (eds.), *The Lost Children*, Sydney: Doubleday, pp. ix–xvii.

Rose, Deborah Bird (1989). 'Remembrance', *Aboriginal History* 13, 1–2, pp. 135–48.

Rose, Deborah Bird (1992). 'Hidden Histories', *Island* 51, pp. 14–18.

Roughsey, Elsie (Labumore) (1984). *An Aboriginal Mother Tells of the Old and the New*, Melbourne: McPhee Gribble/Penguin.

Rowse, Tim (l993a). *After Mabo: Interpreting Indigenous Traditions*, Melbourne: Melbourne University Press.

Rowse, Tim (1993b). 'The Aboriginal Subject in Autobiography: Ruby Langford's *Don't Take Your Love to Town*', *Australian Literary Studies* 16, 1, pp. 14–29.

Schaffer, Kay and Sidonie Smith (2004). "Conjunction: Life Narratives in the Field of Human Rights', *Biography* 27, 1, pp. 1–24.

Scott, Kim (2011). 'Can You Anchor a Shimmering Nation State via Regional Indigenous Roots? Kim Scott talks to Anne Brewster about *That Deadman Dance*', *Cultural Studies Review*, 18, 1, pp. 4–21.

Simon, Ella (1978). *Through My Eyes*, Adelaide: Rigby.

Smith, Shirley (1977). 'Shirley Smith', in Kevin Gilbert (ed.), *Living Black*, Ringwood: Penguin, pp. 246–51.

Smith, Shirley with Bobbi Sykes (1981). *Mum Shirl*, Melbourne: Heinemann.

Smith, Sidonie and Julia Watson (2010). *Reading Autobiography*, 2nd ed. Minneapolis: University of Minnesota Press.

Spivak, Gayatri Chakravorty (1987). *Other Worlds: Essays in Cultural Politics*, New York and London: Methuen.

Sykes, Roberta (1984). 'Bobbi Sykes', in Robyn Rowland (ed.), *Women Who Do and Women Who Don't Join the Women's Movement,* Melbourne: Routledge and Kegan Paul, pp. 63-9.

Sykes, Roberta (1991). 'Black Women and the Continuing Struggle for Resources', in Dale Spender (ed.), *Heroines,* Ringwood: Penguin, pp. 180-6.

Tarrago, Isabel (1993). 'Response to Sally Morgan and the Construction of Aboriginality', *Australian Historical Studies* 25, 100, pp. 469.

Tucker, Margaret (1977). *If Everyone Cared,* Sydney: Ure Smith.

van den Berg, Rosemary (1994). *No Options. No Choice!,* Broome: Magabala.

van den Berg, Rosemary (1995) 'The Cultural Diversity of Aborigines in Australia', *Museums West* 8, 1, March, pp. 8-9.

Walker, Della and Tina Coutts (1989). *Me and You,* Canberra: Aboriginal Studies Press.

Ward, Glenyse (1988). *Wandering Girl,* Broome: Magabala.

Ward, Glenyse (1991). *Unna You Fullas,* Broome: Magabala.

West, Ida (1987). *Pride Against Prejudice,* rev. ed., Canberra: Australian Institute of Aboriginal Studies.

West, Russell (2003). 'Uncovering Collective Crimes: Sally Morgan's My Place as Australian Indigenous Detective Narrative', in *Sleuthing Ethnicity: The Detective in Multiethnic Crime Fiction,* Dorothea Fischer-Hornung, Monika Mueller Danvars (eds.) New Jersey: Rosemont Publishing and Printing Corp., pp. 280-297.

Westphalen, Linda (2012). *An Anthropological and Literary Study of Two Aboriginal Women's Life Histories: The Impacts of Enforced Child Removal and Policies of Assimilation,* New York: Edwin Mellen Press.

Whitlock, Gillian (2001). 'In the Second Person: Narrative Transactions in Stolen Generations Testimony' *Biography,* 24, 1, Winter, pp. 197-214.

Whitlock, Gillian (2015). *Postcolonial Life Narratives: Testimonial Transactions,* Oxford: Oxford University Press.

Winch, Tara June (2006). *Swallow the Air,* St Lucia, Qld.: University of Queensland Press.

www.ingramcontent.com/pod-product-compliance
Lightning Source LLC
Chambersburg PA
CBHW062120080426
42734CB00012B/2928